HAUNTED DETROIT

NICOLE BEAUCHAMP

Haunted America

Published by Haunted America
A Division of The History Press
Charleston, SC
www.historypress.com

Front and back cover photos copyright of Amy Shabluk.
Opposite: *Courtesy of Phil Conners*.

First published 2022

Manufactured in the United States

ISBN 9781467150606

Library of Congress Control Number: 2022936606

Notice: The information in this book is true and complete to the best of our knowledge. It is offered without guarantee on the part of the author or The History Press. The author and The History Press disclaim all liability in connection with the use of this book.

This book is dedicated to the memory of Edward "Ed" C. Steele Jr. He deeply loved Detroit and the city's diverse population. He dedicated all his spare time to restoring the former Detroit Police 6th Precinct building. It is my hope that his dream of reviving Detroit's neighborhoods and historic buildings will continue in his honor via community efforts.

CONTENTS

ACKNOWLEDGEMENTS

A huge thank-you to John Rodrigue from Arcadia Publishing for making this project possible. I appreciate you giving me another opportunity to write more stories about Michigan's most haunted locales. To my late grandparents Alfred and Evelyn Perry, for fostering my love of writing and for having shown me an incredible amount of love throughout my life. I miss you both so much it hurts. To my mother, Ellen; father, Harold; brother, Bruce; Aunt Amy; Aunt Irina; Uncle Rex; Uncle Mike; and cousins Perry, Lauren, Alex, Sasha and Maria. You all inspire me and motivate me to be a better person than I was yesterday. I love you guys so much! To Stephanie Gatza for standing by me through thick and thin and for always supporting my crazy—and sometimes overwhelming—decisions. To Kati Jones, Frances Kermeen, Michelle Blankenship, Carrie and Reanna Crowl, Karen and Kelly Klamer and the wonderful staff at Studio 23 for making me realize just how worthy and capable I actually am. To Bobby Jereb and Amy Shabluk (Portraits by Amy Michelle), for not only going out of your way to help me achieve the highest quality and most attractive images imaginable for this publication but for also being incredible friends to me. I am so fortunate to know you ladies! Thank you to Jay Itchon (Misanthropia Narcissus) for my amazing headshot and phenomenal promotional photos.

Special thanks to the owners, staff and volunteers from the locations I wrote about who assisted me in getting content: Tony Muzzi and Deborah Fuller from The Whitney; the late Ed Steele Jr. from the Historic Detroit 6th Precinct; Stephen Rissman from Elmwood Cemetery; Ed Kachadoorian and Phil Vermeulen from the Historic Fort Wayne Coalition; Jay Itchon from the Leland City Club; and Jason Osterman, Michele Casey, Joe Stanson, Steven Shipp and Ed, Jim and Zac Terebus from Erebus Haunted Attraction. To the paranormal teams and individuals who shared their ghost stories with me: Brian Danhausen of Into the Afterlife Paranormal; Jeff Adkins and Todd Bonner of Detroit Paranormal Expeditions (DPX); David Sartin and Dennis and Maggie Hagan of Toledo Spirit Hunters; Keith Hembree of the Lower Michigan Paranormal Society (LMPS); Marc Ortiz and Ed Kachadoorian of Haunt Investigators of Michigan; Alejandra and Zoë Amalia; Ace Taylor; Deandra Jones; Faith Gearns; Stacy Wright; Rick Frame; Jenny LaBay; Mr. Franklin; Todd Stevenson and everyone else who chose to remain completely anonymous. To the historians, archive collectors, educational faculty and organizations, photographers and friends that provided me with helpful information and abundant resources for the book: Jeremy Dimick and Joel Stone from the Detroit Historical Society; Tyler Moll from the Wayne Historical Museum; Carla Reczek of the Detroit Public Library; Karin Risko of City Tour Detroit; Jeffrey Lemaux of the Detroit Police Museum; Bill Marino at Eastern Michigan University; the Troy Public Library; Mark Bowden and Dawn Eurich at the Burton Historical Collection; Angelo Moreno at the East Lansing Public Library; the Southfield Public Library; Nathaniel Nietering at the State Historic Preservation Office; Adam Oster of the Library of Michigan; the Bay County Library System; Dr. Abdul El-Sayed of Wayne State University; Elizabeth Clemens of the Walter P. Reuther Library (Archives of Labor and Urban Affairs) at Wayne State University; attorney Maurice Davis of Davis Law Group PLLC; Lynda Quirino, Erica Swanson, Phil Conners, Shannon Rodriguez, John E.L. Tenney, Tim Steele and Roxanne Rhoads.

I want to thank everyone who picked up this book and gave it a chance. Your support means so much to me! I also want to acknowledge the paranormal community and the remainder of my friends, extended family and social media followers who have continually motivated me, encouraged me and shown up for my events since 2009. I would not be here without you. Lastly, I want to give a shout-out to anyone out there who has ever doubted themselves, fallen on hard times or been made to believe that their goals are just pipe dreams. I am living proof of someone who has risen from the ashes. Never give up, and do not let anyone tell you that you cannot do something. You can do anything you set your mind to with enough hard work and perseverance. If you internalize anything out of my book, let it be this quote by Layne Beachley: "There are so many people out there who will tell you that you can't. What you've got to do is turn around and say, 'Watch me.'"

PREFACE

DISCLAIMER: In the text, historic quotes are used verbatim that are not considered politically correct. However, they do not reflect the views or opinions of the author. These quotes reflect the perspective of the era in which the story is set. A few names within the book have been slightly modified at the request of the contributors to protect their privacy. In addition, graphic and disturbing descriptions of violence, murder, suicide, abuse, death, social injustice and mistreatment of animals and children are present in the book and may be upsetting to some individuals and unsuitable for younger readers.

Only three suspected apparition photographs were captured at Historic Fort Wayne in Detroit, Michigan. I was the photographer of one of those photos. I remember the night I took the photo as if it were yesterday—the date was October 31, 2009. A little over three months after starting my paranormal team, Tri-City Ghost Hunters Society, the group wanted to branch out of our hometown and nearby cities and investigate something grander. After performing an internet search for something fun to do on Halloween, we discovered that a paranormal team local to the Detroit area was offering overnight ghost hunts at a historic fort that was built in the early 1840s to protect Americans from British invasion after the War of 1812. Arrangements were made for our team to visit, and when the day arrived, we headed downstate to see this historic marvel for ourselves.

As daylight turned to nightfall, two female investigators and I stationed ourselves in the powder magazine of the second casemate from the entrance of the fort. I was crouched down in front of my fellow teammates, snapping photos repeatedly with my brand-new Kodak digital camera. The flash from my camera was the only source of light in the pitch-black tunnel that we were in. Snapping each photo, I glanced down to monitor if any activity was being captured. After taking about twenty-five photos of the empty tunnel in front of me, filled with nothing but orbs of dust and debris, I began to lose hope that I would capture anything worthy. We were just about to pack up our gear and head to another area of the fort when I told myself, *Come on, just take one more photo.* Reluctantly, I snapped the twenty-sixth photo and glanced down at the LCD panel. Noticing the form of a person at the end of the tunnel on my camera, I zoomed in on the screen and, sure enough, could make out a dark figure standing there facing us while leaned up against the bricks of the tunnel. While this figure was dark, it was also shadowy and translucent. Illuminating my flashlight as fast as humanly possible, I bolted out toward the entrance of the casemate looking for whoever or whatever was in there with us. There was no one to be found. What was additionally eerie was knowing how difficult entering and exiting the casemate was, even in broad daylight, due to the winding, uneven steps. In the extreme darkness, climbing the steps, especially quickly, was practically impossible without risking serious injury.

Since a photo of this nature is extremely rare, it caught the attention of Fort Wayne's resident paranormal team, as well as members of the Historic Fort Wayne Coalition. Members from both organizations came to examine the exact spot where I had photographed the mysterious shadow figure. Upon analyzing the photo and the area where the photo was taken for hours upon hours, we had all concluded that the figure was a Civil War soldier clad in a kepi and sturdy boots. Based on the bricks that we had counted, we discovered that he was just over five feet tall, which was a standard height for men during that era. The photo soon made its rounds all over Detroit, the state of Michigan and the whole of the United States. It was featured on a plethora

Author Nicole Beauchamp captured a shadow figure, believed to be a Civil War soldier, in the powder magazine of the second casemate on Halloween 2009. The photo made national news. *Author photo.*

of regional and national television programs, newspapers and magazines. It even graced the desk of *Ghost Hunters* star Grant Wilson, who publicly acknowledged that he believed the photograph was authentic evidence of the paranormal. While this was no doubt a surreal and thrilling experience so early on in my paranormal career, it inspired me to make Historic Fort Wayne a mainstay on our paranormal investigation schedule. We visited the fort countless times for investigations and events between 2009 and 2014, when the commercial paranormal hunts came to an end due to policy changes within the coalition.

Over the course of those five years, Detroit became like a second home to me. I fell in love with Detroit's beautiful and deserted structures and the city's friendly locals. I was regaled often with spooky stories and urban legends from locations all over the city and surrounding area. As a new paranormal investigator finding my place in the paranormal community, something I had dreamt of ever since I was a little girl, Historic Fort Wayne helped me find the spirit of Detroit in more ways than one.

BEWARE THE NAIN ROUGE, DETROIT'S DEVIL OF DOOM

The city of Detroit is best known internationally as the "Motor City Capital of the World." On June 4, 1896, in the wee hours of the morning, automotive pioneer Henry Ford debuted his first attempt at a gasoline-powered vehicle, the quadricycle, from the shed behind his Bagley Avenue home. He even test-drove it down the streets of "the D," as the city is lovingly nicknamed. For decades, Detroit housed three of the largest and most successful automotive companies in the world: Ford Motor Company, General Motors and Chrysler. Although the city's automobile history is quite impressive, the auto industry is just one facet of Detroit's fame.

Detroit has much to brag about: the born and bred musical talents of Motown legends and international recording artists, such as Diana Ross and the Supremes, the Temptations, Smokey Robinson, Aretha Franklin, Stevie Wonder, Eminem, Kid Rock, Big Sean and Lizzo, just to name a few; various brands catering to those with a sweet tooth, including Faygo and Vernors soda pops, Better Made potato chips and Kar's Nuts; and exceptional animal care facilities like the Detroit Zoo, the Belle Isle Nature Center and the Belle Isle Aquarium.

The city even assisted those fleeing slavery, as it was the last stop on the Underground Railroad. It allowed approximately twenty-five to thirty thousand formerly enslaved individuals to flee to Detroit's neighboring Ontario, Canada, which had abolished slavery by 1833. Detroit was also a notable location for civil rights activism, as it hosted one of the largest civil rights marches, the Walk to Freedom. It was at this event that Martin

Detroit's skyline between 1910 and 1930. *Courtesy of Detroit Publishing Company photograph collection (Library of Congress) Library of Congress Control Number: 2016797119, Reproduction Number: LC-DIG-det-4a27659.*

Luther King Jr. marched down Woodward Avenue and debuted parts of his iconic "I Have a Dream" speech. Civil rights leader and hero Rosa Parks adopted Detroit as her home in August 1957, almost two years after she refused to give up her bus seat to a white man. After her passing, she was buried at Woodlawn Cemetery. The beauty of Detroit is found in its diverse population and cultures. A local organization, Rise Up Detroit, continues to educate, promote and advocate for racial equality and justice.

Detroit boasts one of the biggest theater districts in the United States. Musicals, concerts, conventions and events teeming with attendees are a common theme for Detroit. In addition to an incredible music scene, the city has an enormous sports culture and is home to the Detroit Tigers, Lions, Pistons and Red Wings. But beyond the screams of excitement from the Little Caesars Arena, Comerica Park and Ford Field are screams of terror.

One of the oldest and most feared legends that haunts the city of Detroit is that of the Nain Rouge, which in French means "red dwarf." This frightening creature, which is known by many names—the "Demon of the Strait," the "Devil of Detroit" and the "Red Imp"—is believed to be the harbinger of doom. Sightings of this cursed demon predate the European hamlet established on July 24, 1701. The horrifying red-faced imp with its childlike frame, glowing eyes and razor-sharp teeth first appeared in French explorer Antoine de la Mothe Cadillac's nightmares just prior to his establishment of the city of Detroit. The repeated visions included a small red devil sabotaging Cadillac's hopes and aspirations for his newly discovered territories. It was not until Cadillac met a fortune-teller by the name of Mother Minique that he was able to make sense of his disturbing dreams. She tried to protect him from the curse of the Nain Rouge, so long as he heeded her warnings. But let us go back to the beginning.

On March 5, 1658, Detroit's founder, Antoine Laumet, was born to middle-class parents, Jean Laumet (a provincial magistrate) and Jeanne Péchagut, in southern France. In 1683, Antoine headed to Port Royal—now Annapolis Royal, Nova Scotia—at the age of twenty-five. After settling there, he dedicated years of his life working aboard a ship to protect the Acadian coasts against the British. During his service at sea, he became an expert on the coastline of New France and submitted in-depth reports and maps to the French government to assist in protecting the French territories of the New World.

One ship on which he served was captained by privateer François Guyon. Antoine established a good business relationship and friendship with Guyon and visited his family frequently while he was in Quebec. During the visits, Antoine developed a romantic interest in Guyon's niece Marie-Thérèse Guyon and finally married her on June 25, 1687, in Beauport, Quebec City. During his marriage, Antoine claimed to be a member of the French nobility. The *Canadian Encyclopedia* disclosed that Antoine had fabricated his family's status and upbringing to appear far more prestigious than he was by stating the following, "I am Antoine de la Mothe, horseman, esquire de Cadillac, 26 years of age, son of Jean de la Mothe, lord of the said Cadillac, of Launay and of Montet, counsel to the Parliament of Toulouse, and [son] of Lady Jeanne de Malenfant." His marriage certificate was the first documentation that bore his self-given name.

With this honorable social status, the newly proclaimed Cadillac soon began his rise to fame and fortune. He gained the trust and respect of the French government for compiling documentation of the North American continent. In 1688, he and his wife returned to Acadia to start a family, as Cadillac was granted land by New France's Governor Jacques-René de Brisay in what would later become Bar Harbor, Maine. Throughout his marriage, Cadillac fathered a total of thirteen children. Things seemed to be going his way, and his military career began presenting him with new opportunities. In 1693, Cadillac accepted the title of commandant of Fort Michilimackinac. As commandant, he managed fur trades between Michigan, Ohio, Missouri and Mississippi. Cadillac's position was of great importance during this era, as the Beaver Wars were intensifying between the French and the Iroquois Native Americans due to extremely competitive fur trading and desires for land expansion. Cadillac's role as commandant was not without controversy. He became enthralled with becoming as wealthy as possible and participated in trading furs and selling alcohol for his own benefit. His greed, combined with a lack of military planning, made him a questionable choice for the position. Cadillac had such a one-track mind when it came to profiting from trades, he desired to colonize a portion of New France referred to as Pays-d'en-Haut, which was, unsurprisingly, a trading hot spot among voyageurs. The location sat along a body of water known as *le détroit*, which means "the strait" in English. This waterway is now known as the Detroit River. In 1698, Cadillac made his way back to France so that he could request King Louis XIV's permission to establish a French outpost. Two years later, in 1700, after much convincing by Cadillac, French naval minister Jérôme Phélypeaux Comte de Pontchartrain approved the establishment of a settlement.

After returning from France, Cadillac attended a party thrown in his honor on the evening of March 10, 1701. Cadillac, in the company of French soldiers, sat mingling and laughing around a dinner table set with expensive silver and glistening crystal as chamber music echoed down the hallways of an elegant old castle in St. Louis, Quebec. The men had high hopes for their newly awarded French settlement, which would be named after the naval minister who granted them the land. They called the territory "Detroit." A servant quietly entered the joyous room to inform the host of the party that a fortune-teller was outside and desired to enter. With permission, she was allowed in. As the elderly sorceress entered the room, the men gasped in amazement at her off-kilter appearance, complete with rapidly moving eyes that glinted against her deep olive complexion and bizarre raggedy attire. A scraggly black cat sat perched upon her left shoulder. One of the men asked her to reveal her name. "They call me Mother Minique, the witch," she replied in a raspy tone with a Hungarian accent. She went through the group of outstretched hands, reading palms. Finally, she reached the palm of Antoine de la Mothe Cadillac. Initially skeptical of her abilities, he asked her to reveal his future. As detailed in the 1883 book *Legends Le Detroit* by Marie Caroline Watson Hamlin, the revelation unfolded as follows: "Sieur, yours is a strange destiny. A dangerous journey you will soon undertake; you will found a great city which one day will have more inhabitants than New France now possesses; many children will nestle around your fireside."

After a moment of silence, Cadillac encouraged her to tell him more about the fate that awaited him. Reluctantly, she continued:

> *Mon Chevalier, I wish you had not commanded me to go on, for dark clouds are arising and I see dimly your star. The policy you intend pursuing in selling liquor to the savages, contrary to the advice of the Jesuits, will cause you much trouble, and be the cause of your ruin. In years to come your colony will be the scene of strife and bloodshed. The Indians will be treacherous, the hated English will struggle for its possession, but under a new flag it will reach a height of prosperity which you never in your wildest dreams pictured. You will bask in a sunnier climate, but France will claim your last sigh.*

Cadillac had one last burning question for the fortune-teller: "Will my children inherit my possessions?" It was at this time that Mother Minique issued a warning: "Your future and theirs lie in your own hands, beware of undue ambition; it will mar all your plans. Appease the Nain Rouge! Beware of offending him. Should you be thus unfortunate not a vestige of your inheritance will be given to your heirs. Your name will be scarcely known in the city you founded." Cadillac later laughed off the readings, but his wife found the predictions to be no laughing matter.

On June 5, 1701, one hundred people headed from Montreal, Quebec, to the area that would soon be developed into Detroit. On July 24, 1701, the group finally arrived on the Western Bank of the Detroit River. By 1707, the population of the settlement had grown. Cadillac believed that the inhabitants of the land had minor struggles in terms of conflict or taxes, and overall, they seemed content. Unabashedly prideful of his growing legacy and the amount of wealth he had amassed in such a short period of time, he thought life was grand and could not foresee any threats on the horizon.

One warm spring evening, as the sun began to set, Cadillac and his wife decided to go for an evening stroll. On their walk, they overheard two boisterous men complaining about the oppression and injustices they faced as impoverished citizens of the colony. One of the men vented loudly about how the wealthy had everything handed to them on a silver platter, while the poor were exploited financially. His friend's response was that things would not continue this way forever, as only a few days ago, his wife had spotted a little red man. As the two men wandered in the opposite direction of Cadillac and his wife, their conversation trailed off, becoming inaudible. Cadillac's wife, in realization of what was said, clutched her husband's hand in a panic. Looking up at him with fear-stricken eyes, she explained that the little red man the two men were discussing just a few moments prior was indeed the heinous Nain Rouge. Laughing off what he believed was just his wife's overactive imagination, Cadillac suggested they head back to the comfort of their home. Deep down, Cadillac did not want to admit it, but he could feel his apprehension building. He remained speechless until the duo spotted a frightening figure of unusually small stature quickly approaching them on the path. In the twilight, they could make out that the creature had clammy red skin, glowing scarlet eyes and an evil grin that showcased long, needle-like teeth. Startled by the figure's grotesque appearance, Cadillac's first reaction was to strike the freakish being with his cane and scare it away. "Get out of my way!" Cadillac shouted. The creature laughed maniacally before disappearing into the distance. The curse of the Nain Rouge was set in motion, and Cadillac's life soon began its downward spiral.

King Louis XIV caught wind of unethical practices by Cadillac, including, but not limited to, falsifying records about the population of his settlement, trading with and bribing the English and distributing alcohol. Cadillac and his troops were ordered back to Montreal, where he was arrested for extortion and abuse of power. Pontchartrain further punished Cadillac by sending him to govern Louisiana, which was the most financially destitute of all the French colonies. The conditions of work were bleak and miserable. In 1716, not long into his position as governor, he was ordered to return to France. When he arrived in Paris in the fall of 1717 with his son at his side, both men were thrown into the Bastille on suspicions of treason. They spent a total of six lonely months behind bars. In October 1730, Cadillac died a man of limited means in Castelsarrasin, France. Only three of Cadillac's thirteen children survived him, and not one of them received an inheritance.

Nain Rouge sightings in Detroit have spanned hundreds of years, almost always preceding tragic, historic events within the city. On July 30, 1763, the creature was seen the day before the Battle of Bloody Run, where masses of English soldiers were massacred. He was spotted ahead of the Great Fire of 1805 that raged uncontrollably throughout the city of Detroit. During the War of 1812, General William Hull, an American military officer, caught a glimpse of the foul beast snickering at him as he relinquished the city of Detroit to the British. He became the only person on record sentenced to death for military incompetence.

Sixty years later, another possible Nain Rouge sighting made headlines. It was a chilly Wednesday evening in the late 1800s. Jane Dacy was tidying up at her residence on East Elizabeth Street when she entered a dimly lit room to do chores. Upon entering the room, her eyes fell upon a disturbing specter resembling a demon. In a moment of sheer terror, she collapsed unconscious onto the floor. After coming to, Jane reported the entity as having "blood-red eyes, long teeth and rattling hoofs." Following the sighting, Jane was so traumatized by what she had seen in her home that she became physically ill and remained in her bed the following day. A *Detroit Free Press* article dated October 11, 1872, detailed the account.

The goblin made an appearance just prior to the Detroit Rebellion of 1967, in which many people were left unemployed, homeless and dealing with widespread racism. One of the last reported sightings was witnessed on March 1, 1976, when two DTE Energy linemen saw what they assumed was a child climbing an electric pole. Upon closer inspection, they gasped in horror as the red mischief-maker leapt from the pole and took off into the distance. The next day, the Great Ice Storm of 1976 devastated the city.

An annual Mardi Gras–esque parade, the Marche du Nain Rouge, gathers every spring to rid the city of the malevolent dwarf for another year. Above and beyond chasing the nain away, the gathering symbolizes that nothing can or will ever destroy the resilience of Detroiters. Some believe in the Nain Rouge wholeheartedly, some believe the tale is nothing more than a myth and some believe his presence is simply misunderstood. Whatever you believe, if you see a peculiar-looking red goblin trotting down the streets of Detroit, disaster is near.

CORRUPTION, CASE FILES
AND CREEPS

It started out as a regular uneventful Saturday in the summer of 2016. A garage sale was being held at the former Detroit Police Department's 6th Precinct Station to raise funds for providing much-needed repairs and renovations to the building. Ed Steele Jr., the building's owner and founder of the Historic Detroit 6th Precinct Restoration Project, hired five individuals (two women and three men) from the surrounding neighborhood to assist him with the sale. After a full day of working the sale and hauling heavy tables, doors, windows, plywood and various other large materials back and forth, everyone was feeling exhausted. The four fatigued men, including Ed, continued to pack up for the night. Despite sounds of passing traffic, the neighborhood was peaceful, and the soft breeze drifting through the open doors and windows felt nice after a long day in the sun. All was going well, until Ed heard bloodcurdling shrieks coming from the basement. In a panicked state, Ed instantly dropped what he was doing and ran downstairs, the three men trailing after him. When they got to the basement, there stood the two female workers in a state of hysteria. "He touched my hair! He touched me!" one of the women repeatedly screamed. The other woman shoved her iPhone into Ed's face. "I caught it on camera. Look!"

Ed stood confused about what was going on. As he was trying to process what had just occurred, all five workers looked at one another wide-eyed and bolted out of the basement, never to be seen or heard from by Ed again.

The story of how the former 6th Precinct Station came to be dates all the way back to the turn of the century. In the year 1900, Detroit had a population

Courtesy of Jeffrey Lemaux of the Detroit Police Museum.

of 285,704. Many manufacturers set up their factories alongside the Detroit River, which proved to be extremely convenient for importing and exporting. A plethora of industries flocked to the area, including the automobile industry, pharmaceuticals, tobacco products, rail cars, shipbuilding, breweries, foundries and machine shops. The automotive industry was relatively small at the start of the twentieth century but was steadily growing.

On June 16, 1903, Henry Ford—along with twelve others and an investment of $28,000—established the Ford Motor Company. Ford, on a mission to build a vehicle that would be reliable, reasonably priced and easy to maneuver, introduced the first Model T to the world in 1908. Soon the company was being inundated with orders for the new car. The American industrialist put his revolutionary vision for the Ford Motor Company in motion and commissioned the first large automobile manufacturing plant in Highland Park, Michigan. It was here in 1913 that Ford implemented the first moving assembly line for cars, which dropped production time for creating the vehicles from over twelve hours to only one hour and thirty-three minutes. This incredible invention catapulted Ford to the forefront of the auto industry. On January 5, 1914, Henry Ford and James Couzens, the company's vice president, made international headlines when they shockingly announced that the Ford Motor Company would begin paying male employees a whopping $5.00 a day for eight hours of factory work as opposed to $2.34 for nine hours of factory work. While there is much historical speculation about why this was done or if Ford's heart was in the right place, this huge increase in pay led to a better standard of living for the workers and a much lower turnover rate. People from all over the world flocked to the city of Detroit to work for Ford, causing Detroit's population to expand.

By 1925, automobile manufacturing had begun to decline, yet by 1929, the number of people living in Detroit had jumped to 1.6 million. Americans across the country were engaging in wide-scale consumption of domestic appliances and products via the use of credit or installment payments. This way of living proved to be highly unsustainable. In addition to this frivolous spending, the stock market crashed on October 29, 1929, which largely affected the wealthy. As banks failed and businesses closed all over the United States, over 15 million employees lost their jobs. So, while the crash alone did not cause the Great Depression, it was most certainly a contributing factor to the fall of the American and Detroit economies.

In November 1929, President Herbert Hoover requested that business owners meet him at the White House to ensure that they would not reduce their employees' wages. Hoover thought if people's wages remained unchanged that they could continue consuming goods and services and that could possibly help to improve the economy. Private companies promised the president that in 1930 they would collectively put $1.8 billion toward developing new facilities that would create an abundance of construction jobs and improve the country's infrastructure. The president directed federal agencies to accelerate construction efforts and directed all governors to extend public works projects in their respective states. Hoover requested that Congress honor a tax cut of $160 million, while at the same time allocating increased funds for dams, harbors, highways and public buildings. A new police precinct serving southwest Detroit was ordered to be built at 6840 McGraw Avenue, replacing the station located at 3545 Vinewood Street. The building was completed by the fall of 1930. The thick walls of the historic 6th Precinct, also known as the McGraw Station and, later, the Gang Squad Headquarters, harbor many secrets. Suicide. Murders. Corruption. The 26,274-square-foot limestone and brick structure stood witness to it all for seventy-five years.

When Ed Steele Jr., who migrated to the Detroit area from Florida in 1994, began searching for a sturdy facility to host his cloud computing

The new McGraw Station announced in the Detroit Police Department's 1930–31 newsletter. *Courtesy of Carla Reczek, Detroit Public Library.*

data center, he never imagined he would own a haunted building, let alone wind up on Travel Channel's *Most Terrifying Places*. When he got wind that the City of Detroit was going to spend $1 million to demolish the historic McGraw Station, he contacted the city straightaway, as the location was perfect for his intended purposes. After eighteen months of negotiations, the city allowed Ed to buy the building in October 2013 for an affordable rate, so long as he honored a list of commitments that would benefit the community. Ed accepted and agreed to transform the historic property into a community event center and employ at-risk youth and other vulnerable members of society. When Ed first set foot inside to begin restoration efforts in the fall of 2014, he was amazed at the poor condition of the building. Since it had been a vandalized trap house for nine years, Ed no doubt had his work cut out for him. Trees were growing out of the bathroom; three feet of water flooded the basement; and heaps of old case files, mug shots, bullets, shells and drug paraphernalia filled the arraignment room, located just inside the front entrance. When Ed began cleaning up the property, he filled a total of forty-two dumpsters with trash and various tubs full of abandoned police records.

Ed continued to question why the staff he had first hired for the precinct's fundraising garage sale had run out on him. While Ed was annoyed at the sudden departure of his staff, he was intrigued by the unusual behavior. He finally reached out to his friend Phil Conners, who suggested his location might be plagued with paranormal activity and arranged for Todd Bonner and Jeff Adkins of Detroit Paranormal Expeditions (DPX) to conduct the first-ever paranormal investigation at the precinct. On a frigid winter evening in 2016, DPX made their first visit to the building.

While beginning their walkthrough of the property, they descended into the basement. Shortly after being down there, they began getting pelted by rocks from an unseen force. The duo specified that the rocks were not simply falling but instead were being hurled at them from across the room with

Graffiti depicting the building's past and modern-day political views. *Author photo.*

so much strength that they could feel the impact of each hit through their thick winter coats. A bit later, Todd decided to check out the evidence room for himself. The evidence room is a lengthy room in the basement adjacent to the precinct's firing range. As he entered the room, he became visibly discomfited. It did not take long before he became enveloped in a thick energy. The door then closed with a bang, trapping Todd inside the room with no way out. Spooked, Todd called Jeff down to help him. After what seemed like an eternity of prying the door open, a terror-stricken Todd, finally free from the confines of the evidence room, raced up the stairs. During the night, Todd had also experienced whistling in the jail. Upon searching the entire cell block, he could not locate where the whistling was coming from. The team ended up capturing various voices on their recorders inside the facility. One of the most goosebump-inducing responses was recorded in the evidence room and was captured using a P-SB7 spirit box, which is a device believed to contact the dead via radio frequency. After asking a string of questions trying to elicit a response, Jeff finally asked, "Did you kill yourself in this room?" and a deep male voice replied, "Buddy did." After an active night at the station, the team headed home to upload their paranormal evidence onto their website, which drew nationwide interest in the precinct. Teams from all over the country began calling Ed to set up investigations and experienced activity in some of the same areas of the building that DPX did. When Dennis Hagan and his crew, Toledo Spirit Hunters, drove up from Ohio to check out the claims of activity, they also encountered activity in the cell block. David Sartin, one of Dennis's teammates, saw, with his own eyes, a gangly dark figure pacing back and forth at the entrance of the jail. After an abundance of other paranormal teams posted evidence from their hunts, Travel Channel reached out to Ed to be on a show.

With dozens of paranormal teams capturing evidence at his location, Ed continued to wonder why. He finally decided to pay a visit to local libraries and archives in search of answers. It was then that he made both historical and gruesome discoveries relating to the building's past. He found proof of at least four police officers who took their own lives in the evidence room. He located records indicating that at least twelve inmates died in the jail cells. He read the horrendous details of an officer who shot his wife on the precinct steps and then entered the station to shoot himself in the head for what he had done. Last, but not least, he learned of a prisoner who was cuffed upstairs and had fallen out of the center window of the facility, splitting his head open like an egg on the steps below. The walls of the precinct also bore witness to shady bribes between police officers and the Purple

The jail at the former Detroit Police 6th Precinct building. *Author photo.*

Gang (the most vicious and bloodthirsty gang of the Prohibition era), a mass termination of the station due to corrupt practices and the 1967 Uprising, which was the result of racial profiling and police brutality. Ed even came across a photo of snipers opening fire on the McGraw Station. A place filled with so much violence was bound to have some sort of tormented energy.

Above: The evidence room where many police officers took their own lives. *Author photo.*

Opposite, top: National Guardsmen are pinned down by gunfire at the McGraw Police Station in Detroit's 6th Precinct. *Courtesy of Walter P. Reuther Library, Archives of Labor and Urban Affairs, Wayne State University.*

Opposite, bottom: The McGraw Station back when it was in operation. *Courtesy of Jeffrey Lemaux of the Detroit Police Museum.*

Given the building's rich history, Ed ultimately teamed up with Karin Risko, director of City Tour Detroit, so that the public could come investigate the precinct with seasoned paranormal investigators. Detroiter and paranormal investigator Ace Taylor, who had been volunteering at the precinct since 2016, was on many of those cases. He attributed many different entities to the building. In the basement is the spirit of an angry, cynical man who hates visitors. In the cell block is something evil that barks orders at those who dare to enter. Near the doorway of the basketball court is an entity who communicates only in Spanish. And that is just a glimpse of those who haunt the facility. One of the most common findings by investigations, and most perplexing, was that of an adolescent by the name of "Billy." The name had been captured by many different investigators over the years in all parts of the building, and the presence usually responds

most to words like "pain," "fire" and "help." For years, Ace and Ed both sat scratching their heads over the link between this young boy and the police station. On November 14, 2020, a police officer who worked at the precinct in the 1980s came by for one of the paranormal tours. As he overheard Ed and Karin discussing the mystery of Billy and why the child was associated with the station, the police officer chimed in. "I know Billy."

It was December 17, 1985. It was a week before Christmas break, and two brothers, aged nine and twelve, were living with their mother and her new husband in Taylor, Michigan. The boys had originally grown up in a two-story house on the 4200 block of Lawndale Street in Detroit and longed to go back over holiday break. "Mom, can we please go stay at the old house for a few days to see our friends?" they asked. "Of course!" the mom replied, hugging her two sons.

Their old home was in a slightly compromised state, as it was currently undergoing renovations by the mother's new husband and was being rented by a man and woman with a volatile relationship. One night while the man was gone, the woman left and never returned, not bothering to pay the rent. Because she had disappeared, there was no way of evicting her. Her boyfriend, whose name was not on the lease, remained as an occupant in the home. Because of the growing unpaid rent expenses, he was ordered to leave the property summarily. The first thing he said as he walked out the door was, "If I can't live here, nobody can."

The mother, relieved to see this troublemaker leaving her property, carried on in assisting the boys with setting up the house for their short stay. They arranged mattresses on the floor in the living room. Her husband, who had spent a lot of time at the home, had a bedroom set up upstairs. After an exciting day of being back in their childhood home and seeing their friends, the boys fell fast asleep on their makeshift beds.

Around midnight, the boys were awakened by the sound of shattering glass in the room where they were sleeping. The former tenant who had threatened their mother firebombed the home through the living room window, setting the house ablaze without a moment's notice. The boys raced to the front door at once but found themselves locked behind an anti-theft door. As their stepfather attempted to race down the stairs to get the children, he stumbled backward in shock as he saw flames raging through the living room. With the key to the front door in his pocket, he frantically raced back up the stairs and broke an upstairs window. Thinking that the four inches of fresh snow on the ground below would cushion his fall, he climbed out the window and slid down the icy roof. Upon hitting the ground, he broke his back in three places and lay paralyzed on the snowy lawn. The pocket that had the key to the anti-theft door ripped off his pants from the broken window and the key fell somewhere in the snow, never to be seen again. Neighbors raced over to help the two youngsters, to no avail. The tortured screams of the boys crying for their lives haunted everyone who witnessed it.

The fire continued to spread, engulfing the entire house, and eventually reached one of the boys' pajama bottoms. Two officers from the McGraw Station were driving down Michigan Avenue when they began getting dozens of calls from people in the Lonyo-Michigan Avenue neighborhood that two boys were trapped in a burning house. By error, the cops looked for the address with Lawndale as the cross street, which took them two miles out of the way of the burning house. Time was running out. After seeing a barrage of fire trucks heading in the opposite direction, the police did a U-turn and followed them. Upon arriving at the scene, the officers and neighborhood watched in horror as the two boys burned alive in front of them. After extinguishing the fire, the firemen found the brothers wrapped in each other's arms in the vestibule. The morgue ordered the officers to break the scorched bodies apart with their flashlights to flatten the bones. Feeling responsible for what had happened, crying and apologizing, both officers gently carried out their orders. The stepfather was sent to the Henry Ford Hospital. While neither boy was legally named Billy, the officer indicated that was a nickname for the younger boy. Not long afterward, police began seeing a shadowy young child darting throughout the precinct.

When Ed arrived home at 3:00 a.m. after a long day of tours, he hurriedly pulled up the news article online, verifying the exact story that the officer told him. While searching newspaper archives, Ed also came across another mind-blowing *Detroit Free Press* article titled "These Three Have Nobody Now" from November 13, 1931. Bertha Potenski abandoned her three children—Irene (thirteen), William (twelve) and Edward (ten)—on the streets of Detroit after her husband left her because he could not support the family. Before leaving, she pinned a note on her son William's jacket and instructed him to give it to a policeman. William led his siblings into the McGraw Station, where officers read the note, which requested that the children be fed. The kids were given a hot dinner and then placed in a juvenile detention home while officers located the parents.

Could there possibly be two Billys lingering around the precinct? Former officers and news articles seem to indicate so. While no one can say for sure,

Courtesy of Detroit Free Press *and* Zuma Press.

one thing is for certain—the dreary facility plastered with graffiti is home to a melting pot of spirits. Regardless of the ghostly inhabitants, Ed always remained dedicated to his mission: to restore the old precinct to its original grandeur. On August 25, 2021, the city of Detroit was taken by surprise when a *Crain's Detroit* news article reported that Ed passed away at Beaumont Hospital in Royal Oak at the age of fifty-four. The cause of his death was undisclosed. His legacy now lives on through his children.

THE HOTEL OF HORRORS

Often compared to the Cecil Hotel in Los Angeles, California, the Detroit-Leland Hotel, simply known as the Leland, emits a heaviness that could make even the strongest person weak. Walking down the dimly lit hallways gives you the same feeling that is experienced when you are told a loved one has passed. Perhaps that is because the Leland has been witness to an exceedingly high number of suicides, murders, accidents, acts of violence and overdoses since its opening on April 20, 1927. This towering derelict steel-framed building at 400 Bagley Street has been described as Detroit's portal to hell.

Prior to the Leland being built, all was well, and fairly uneventful, at the northwest corner of Bagley and Cass Avenues. And while maybe it should have stayed that way, Harry Stormfeltz and Edward Loveley, two commercial realtors, had a vision to turn Bagley Avenue from one of downtown's back streets into a bustling hot spot. The Leland Hotel was one of three structures built as part of the Detroit Properties Corporation's Bagley Avenue development project. Chicago architects C.W. and George L. Rapp, known for designing many twentieth-century theaters, were put in charge of designing the Leland.

The building was named after Henry Martyn Leland, an automotive industrialist and founder of two luxury automotive brands: Cadillac and Lincoln. While the hotel was being added to an already established collection of hotels in the city, between the soaring population and growing tourism, more guest rooms were needed. In 1927, the Detroit Convention and Tourist

Left: The exterior of the Leland hides clues about its tragic past. *Courtesy of Amy Shabluk.*

Opposite: Several views of the Detroit-Leland Hotel, including coffee shop, lobby, exterior, dining room, lounge bar and ladies' lounge. *Courtesy of the Burton Historical Collection, Detroit Public Library.*

Bureau reported that within a one-mile radius of downtown Detroit there were approximately twenty-five thousand guest rooms.

When the hotel was first built, it was considered one of the finest in the city. Built at a cost of $4.5 million, the twenty-story Italian Renaissance hotel originally contained 720 guest rooms, each with its own private bathroom and shower. Guests even had access to hot and cold running water. The rooms were advertised as spacious in comparison to competing hotels of the area. The hotel was incredibly opulent, and that was especially showcased in its lobby. Guests could enter the hotel from either the Bagley or Cass Avenue entrances. Upon entering, they would ascend a staircase of black wrought-iron banisters and railings, which led to the main lobby. The guests were greeted by a golden coffered plaster ceiling adorned with brass chandeliers, walls featuring deep hues and oversized

COFFEE SHOP

DINING ROOM and LOUNGE BAR

DETROIT LELAND

THE LOBBY

Detroit-Leland Hotel
Detroit, Michigan

LADIES' LOUNGE

"DETROIT'S NEWEST DOWNTOWN HOTEL"

round arched windows that allowed sunlight to pour in. Fancy period furniture accommodated waiting guests. While air-conditioning units were not developed yet for guest rooms, there was a refrigeration unit used to keep the lobby, ballrooms and dining rooms cool.

Eleven stores were conveniently located on the floor level of the hotel to the left and right of the staircase from the entrance on Bagley Street. There was a barbershop for men and a hair salon for women. A portion of the basement contained a coffee shop. Due to the Leland being built during Prohibition, it initially did not contain any cocktail bars. In the 1930s, when Prohibition finally ended, the Grenadier Dining Room and Lounge Bar was opened in the same area as the storefronts. As time went on, additional bars and nightclubs continued to open on the property as a means to generate more income for the hotel. To serve guests and keep operations running smoothly, 550 employees were hired.

Notoriety is something the Leland will never be able to live down, especially with the local news. On August 14, 1938, George O'Brien was injured after falling from the second floor of the Leland Hotel; September 26, 1942, a salesman by the name of Mark J. Wolff plunged from the twelfth floor of the Leland Hotel to his death; September 15, 1946, Arthur J. Levy was found dead in his bed at the Leland Hotel; July 29, 1949, John Oram Keim plummeted fourteen floors to his death after developing a sleeping pill habit shortly after checking in to the Leland Hotel; January 3, 1966, Dana R. Stair, a grieving father, died by suicide after leaping twelve floors to his death from the Leland Hotel. This is just a fraction of the Leland's macabre past. The stories became more intense, more depressing as time went on. In 1988, a man was shot in the back while walking past the hotel's restaurant, unnerving innocent bystanders. In 2012, a man was found beaten to death inside his apartment at the Leland. In 2016, an eighty-six-year-old man was walking in front of the Leland when a Nemo's Bar Bus crashed into the building, striking the elderly man and leaving him in critical condition. In 2017, a man was in the lobby of the Leland Hotel when he got into an argument with an employee. When security told him to leave the hotel, he refused and was unexpectedly shot by an observer. He was rushed to the hospital in a life-threatening state. Then, in 2018, a man living on the fourteenth floor of the Leland died when his apartment caught fire. Firefighters were unable to get the standpipe system within the complex to work and had to race up fourteen levels of stairs with regular-sized fire extinguishers. The whole building nearly exploded in flames due to the faulty system. With so much tragedy striking in one place, it makes one wonder—is the Leland cursed? Some tend to think so.

Despite its beauty, the hotel's strain of bad luck began when four men lost their lives as the hotel was being built. Not long after, the Leland developed a reputation around Detroit as being a seedy location, as it was frequented by the Purple Gang, which was led by the Bernstein brothers. The gang of ruthless, cold-blooded killers is said to have murdered many people at the Leland by throwing their helpless bodies from the sub-rooftops around the building and making it look accidental. The gang purportedly shot up the lobby at one point. Only two years into the business opening, the Leland's owners experienced serious financial woes that resulted in bankruptcy and lasted until 1936. One year later, on March 6, 1937, the increasing popularity of organizing unions and strikes affected major hotels in the city, including the Leland, and service was suspended until March 17 of that year.

ARTHUR J. LEVY
Found dead in hotel

Hotel Death in City Stirs Police Probe

Courtesy of Detroit Free Press *and* Zuma Press.

Over the course of time, the building endured a variety of transformations and saw a number of different owners. From the 1950s until the early part of the 1960s, Robert, Oliver and Edward Sterling came into ownership of the Leland, and it underwent renovations. In 1959, the Sterlings built a freight elevator into the back of the building that could hold up to a six-ton vehicle, with the intent to host automobile shows. The property changed hands again in 1964, when it was sold to Robert K. and Donald Werbe, who changed the name to the Leland House. They converted 473 units into apartments, and each unit got its very own air conditioner.

In the 1970s, John R. "Jack" Ferris and Detroit attorney Mayer Morganroth bought the property. Ferris belonged to a union group called Teamsters Local 299 and allowed other members to regularly patronize the hotel. This organization was led by James "Jimmy" Riddle Hoffa and was known to be extremely corrupt and violent. Hoffa enjoyed visiting the bar on the fourth floor, the Hideaway Bar, which later became the 400 Bagley Club. In 1975, when Hoffa went missing, the FBI showed up at the Leland House to question Teamster members and search for Hoffa's dead body. Rumor has it, they began their search for him by excavating the basement.

The building was purchased again in 1980 by current owner Michael W. Higgins, who ran the Leland House Limited Partnership Company. Soon after Higgins acquired the building, the recession began seriously affecting businesses downtown, and occupancy was way down from previous years. The hotel suffered great financial loss, and in 1988, it became part of the Ramada hotel chain just to stay afloat.

A gothic nightclub called Liedernacht opened in 1984 and took over the Colonial Ballroom on the second floor, where many mobsters partied. A year later, it was renamed City Club. The striking ballroom was painted black and covered in eldritch art by local artists. In 1998, a dive bar called Dirty Helen's Saloon, in the hotel's basement, was also converted into a gothic club and dubbed the Labyrinth. The Labyrinth eventually closed due to being flooded with sewage. The storefront located at the intersection of Cass and Bagley Avenues served as a variety of restaurants over the years, including Dagwoods and City Bites, as well as Biff's Coffee Shop. A 1950s American-style diner called Lucy and Ethel's currently occupies that space. On July 20, 2005, the hotel was added to the National Register of Historic Places and in 2006 returned to its original name. The owner eventually stopped allowing overnight stays to guests, and the property now serves as low-income housing.

To say that the Leland is creepy would be an understatement. The building is shrouded in mystery from the moment one steps inside the former hotel. The once opulent lobby now sits in a rapidly deteriorating state. The rows of stores sit vacant, a reminder that life and success are fleeting. Security meticulously monitors the traffic to and from the door to the apartments and does not allow photographs to be taken inside the building. While a number of Detroiters call this property home, hardly any residents are ever spotted entering or exiting the premises. If one ever does manage to make it inside the door that leads to the apartments, they will discover just how peculiar the interior is. The elevators are unpredictable and unreliable, often forcing residents to use the stairwells, which are dark and covered in graffiti. The eerily silent hallways to the apartments are poorly lit and marred with dents, holes, paint and questionable stains. Some apartments are occupied by families. Other apartment doors sit wide open with someone's belongings still inside, akin to the homes of Chernobyl. The beds are made, the tables are set and the cabinets are full, but no one is there. It is a particularly unsettling experience peering into these rooms, wondering if the police have hauled the tenants away, if the tenants became victims of their environment, if they just simply stepped outside for a smoke or if squatters are now residing in their units. Some floors sit fully abandoned, and other floors are totally inaccessible. Tarps hang to hide fully abandoned sections of the former hotel from residents. Stairs lead to nowhere. The Leland does not just look like a horror story; the Leland *is* a horror story.

Staff members, residents and guests have reported ghost sightings for almost as long as the building has been standing. Housekeepers have quit and never returned after being called by name in the empty rooms that they were cleaning. Employees of the hotel have heard a piano playing, been grabbed by unseen hands and observed strange figures lingering around the clubs and property during times they were not open to the public. The two most common apparition sightings in the basement include that of a man dressed in a stylish suit and hat awaiting his next drink and a lady in white who curiously watches hotel happenings from the bathroom. Seeing phantom roof jumpers is a phenomenon that has terrorized Detroit for decades.

Jay Itchon, who got his start at the City Club in 2012 and now serves as the resident DJ, has had scads of eerie encounters at the hotel. While working alone, he has often spotted human-like

Grieving Father Leaps to Death

Dana R. Stair, 39, ended nearly two years of grieving for his dead daughter when he leaped to his death Sunday from his 12th floor apartment at the Detroit Leland Hotel, Cass and Bagley.

His wife, Barbara, who was in the apartment when he jumped, collapsed from shock.

The Stairs arrived in Detroit before Christmas from Yardley, Pa.

• • •

STAIR, A SALES engineer for Baldwin-Ehret-Hill, Inc., was despondent over the death of his daughter, Linda, who died at 15 of an incurable congenital disease.

A friend of the family told police that during the Christmas holidays, Stair seemed happy.

But about 1 p.m. Sunday he went to the window, opened it and jumped to the parking lot below.

His wife, unable to talk to police, was placed under sedation.

Where victim leaped
Free Press Photo

Courtesy of Detroit Free Press *and* Zuma Press.

Author Nicole Beauchamp sitting in the club's stairwell, where a lot of tragedy and paranormal activity has been witnessed. *Courtesy of Jay Itchon (Misanthropia Narcissus).*

figures moving about in his peripheral vision. "I always feel like someone is watching me." he said.

The former entrance to the City Club and associated blue-lit graffitied stairwell shares a minacious reputation.

Located in the Leland's parking lot, the former entrance now serves as a side door for cigarette breaks and is believed to be the death site of at least one suicide jumper. Pretty gruesome to think about people socializing, hugging and laughing all in the same exact spot a man's skull was shattered. The stairwell to the dance floor has been known to make otherwise healthy people sick. Allegedly, it has been the location of umpteen killings and attempted murders. For decades, perpetrators have tossed bodies down the stairs as if the victims were nothing but rag dolls. While climbing the staircase, visitors have spotted a monstrous figure with bulging eyes and long disheveled white hair scamper by on all four limbs.

Michigan actor and artist Todd Stevenson was a City Club regular from 2014 through 2016 and even briefly lived at the Leland in 2016. Many early mornings, after club business hours, Todd would sneak up to the upper levels of the hotel that were considered uninhabitable. Every visit to the upper floors resulted in a paranormal experience. Seven-foot-tall apparitions, cold spots and a heavy negative atmosphere left a lasting impression on Stevenson. His worst recollection was that of the overbearing scent of rotting remains. "It smelled like a hot, wet animal decomposing. My family owned Hill Funeral Home in Grand Blanc, and I wanted to go into mortuary science, so I know what death smells like. What I encountered at the Leland actually smelled worse. But I knew it was paranormal, and not real, as it would come and go very quickly."

Detroiter Alejandra Amalia has been to the Leland many times and grew up being told by her mother, who lived there in the 1980s, what a bizarre place it was. One day while her mother was taking the elevator, a woman stepped on the lift with her and pulled out a pair of scissors. The lady proceeded to cut a huge chunk of her own hair off and put it into a plastic baggie with various chunks of other people's locks. Alejandra described the Leland as being "a vortex of negative energy for people that are at the threshold of life and death." One night, Alejandra and her twin sister, Zoë, went out dancing at the City Club with some of their friends to celebrate the life of their dear mutual friend who had passed away. With so much raw emotion there that night, Alejandra felt preyed upon by whoever or whatever possesses the Leland. When she arrived home that night and went to sleep, she experienced an extremely vivid dream in which she was standing on the dance floor at the Leland and a crowd of spirits surrounded her, including her deceased friend. One of the spirits began pleading with Alejandra, "Please get me out of here. I want to go with you. I don't want to be here anymore." So disturbed by the dream she was having, Alejandra jolted awake in a cold sweat. Feeling fearful and unsettled, she texted her sister detailing her dream. A few moments later, Zoë wrote her back stating that both she and their friend Madison, who was also at the Leland the night prior, had the same exact dream that Alejandra had.

YouTube content creator Detroit AllyCat became a regular of the City Club when she was in her twenties. Over the course of time, she developed a positive relationship with Higgins, the owner, and was presented with the opportunity of a lifetime to host some events there. She was ecstatic over the offer, feeling as though she landed her dream job. At the time, the Labyrinth was experiencing a lack of attendance, and the owner knew AllyCat had thrown other events with great turnouts. AllyCat got right to work in preparing for her events by doing some restoration work in the nightclub. While down there painting one night with some friends, she caught wind that no one was allowed to visit the seventh floor and the elevator would not even stop there. After AllyCat convinced the owner to let her see it, one of the managers took her up there via the stairwell. The manager had to move a makeshift wall to allow them access, and when AllyCat stepped onto the floor, she said it was like something right out of the *Silent Hill* video game. All the rooms on that floor looked nearly guest-ready, with people's personal belongings still on the tables, despite the floor being boarded up. Lamps were illuminated inside each room. "It was like time had stopped," AllyCat said. Upon walking up to one of the rooms to peek inside, AllyCat felt a presence overcome her. Although she did not say anything to the manager at the time, he must have felt it too, because he told her they needed to get out of that room. When she finally left her job at the Leland, she even bid the hotel farewell. "I said goodbye to the building like I was talking to a friend. That building has so much of a spirit, it is almost like a person."

Another floor that sits abandoned is the fourth floor, which has been swarming with paranormal activity for decades. Tenants who would take the elevator up to that floor and find that they could not access it could hear men walking around and talking, only to be later told by staff that no one had been allowed up there in years. This floor was Jimmy Hoffa's personal hangout spot, and many people believe his spirit still roams the decaying corridors.

One of the most bone-chilling happenings occurred in the summer of 2008, when Deandra Jones flew to Detroit for a three-week stay with her sister. Although originally born in Detroit, both women now lived across the country from each other and were thrilled that they would be getting to spend some quality time together. "I was so excited to see her, I didn't honestly care if she would have been living in a cardboard box at the time. I just wanted to stay with her and spend time together," Deandra said. She admitted feeling a sense of foreboding when she first entered the Leland but immediately brushed it off as being somewhere new and having a long flight. "I'd never been in there before, and the feeling in there was weird. I cannot really explain it. Just a dark and heavy vibe if that makes sense." The two ladies spent the remainder of the evening laughing, catching up, playing games and having a few drinks. They went to bed and awoke the next morning with nothing notable happening. The next day was jam-packed full of activities, including a trip to the Detroit Zoo and walking around the city reminiscing.

When the ladies arrived back at the apartment around 10:00 p.m., Deandra was exhausted and retired to the bedroom she was staying in, quickly falling into a deep sleep. At midnight she was awakened by the sound of someone choking. Even though it continued for what seemed like forever, she just figured that she was in an apartment complex and her sister's neighbor was likely just a heavy smoker. This continued happening over the course of the next ten nights, always at the exact same time. Finally, on the eleventh night Deandra could not stand it anymore and went out into the hallway to politely ask the neighbor if they could please keep it down and explained that she meant no offense, she was just trying to sleep. As soon as she spoke her piece, the neighbor's choking ceased, and Deandra thanked them and returned to her bed.

When she woke up around 9:00 a.m., she confronted her sister about it. "What's the deal with your neighbor? How do you possibly get any rest in here?" Deandra's sister smiled at her, her head cocked slightly to the side. "What are you talking about, Dee?" Deandra became annoyed. "Come on, girl, don't play with me. I have been hardly getting any sleep here. Every night I am woken up by your neighbor hacking away, and it goes on for the duration of the whole night." Her sister's eyes narrowed on her. "Dee, I don't have any neighbors." Deandra rolled her eyes. "Whatever, girl. I know you are just joking with me, but honestly I'm not in the mood." Deandra's sister led her by her hand out into the hallway. "I'm not playing with you, Dee, and I have no reason to lie to you." Deandra watched in shock as her sister proceeded down the hallway, opening each door as she went, only to reveal that the units were indeed vacant. After overcoming the feelings of surprise, Deandra's logical side took over again. "Well, it's probably just folks sneaking in there then and smoking God knows what." Her sister nodded in agreement, and both women put it behind them so as to not let it impede on their time together.

On the twelfth night, Deandra was up using the restroom when she heard the choking again. When she was finished in the bathroom, she went to her sister's room to shake her awake and tell her it was happening again, but her sister told her to ignore it and just go to sleep. "I don't want any trouble here, Dee," her sister groggily replied before rolling back over into a deep sleep. Deandra had enough at this point and took the elevator down to the lobby to report the disturbance to the front desk staff. After they assured her that they would check it out, Deandra headed back to her sister's apartment. The elevator stopped several floors from where her sister lived, so Deandra reluctantly climbed up the decrepit stairwell, feeling as though someone was trailing behind her. When she reached the floor she was staying on, she began walking toward her sister's apartment when she heard a door slam shut. Startled, she swung around, seeing an unusual, well-dressed man wearing a hat that covered the upper portion of his face standing in front of the door to the stairwell. "What the…who are you?!" she shouted. "You scared me half to death, man!"

As the man tilted his head back to look at her, she noticed he had two bruised eyes that made his greyish complexion look even more ashen. Her eyes trailed down his spooky face to his neck, where she could see what appeared to be a gunshot wound. The man staggered forward, reaching out for Deandra. In a moment of utter panic, Deandra bolted back to her sister's apartment, locking the door behind her and holding the doorknob to make sure it would stay closed. She could hear thudding footsteps in the hallway getting closer to the apartment that she was staying in. *I am losing my mind*, Deandra thought. *I am probably just delirious from lack of sleep.* Deandra, who hardly ever drank, poured herself a glass of straight vodka, which eventually made her tired enough to sleep.

At about 2:00 a.m., Deandra woke up, freezing. When she opened her eyes, she realized her blanket was off her. She yanked her blanket back up to her chin from the bottom of the bed. *I must have just kicked it off myself*, she thought. She glanced around the room, noticing some outside light coming in through the window. Otherwise, nothing was out of the ordinary—that was, until she heard an odd wheezing sound. Glancing around the room once more to see where it was coming from, her eyes met with the vanity that was across from her bed. In the mirror attached to the vanity was a tall, dark silhouette of a man, complete with a hat. "They shot me, and they'll shoot you too," she could hear him whisper in a gravelly tone.

Deandra threw the covers over her head, trembling in fear. She could barely bring herself to breathe as she contemplated what to do. *There is a man in here! Oh my God, there is a man in here!* Deandra's mind ran through many thoughts, ultimately landing on *Is my sister ok?* Just as Deandra was about to muster up enough courage to race from her room to check on her sister, the blanket violently flew off her, and she let out a bloodcurdling shriek. Her sister came racing into the room, flicking on the light switch.

"Deandra! What is wrong? Are you alright?" Her sister dropped to her knees in the room with her hand over her heart. "You scared me so bad, Dee!"

"There's a man in here! Call 911 now!" Deandra scrambled out of the room with her heart pounding.

"No one is in here, Dee. I promise you! No one is in here, just me. You must have just had a bad dream." Her sister went around the apartment flicking on lights in each room to prove that the two women were indeed alone.

Deandra looked at her sister, horrified and with tears in her eyes. "I need to leave. Please come with me back to California. Please. We can work out the arrangements later." Her sister refused, boldly stating that the whole thing was a nightmare and firmly told Deandra that she was losing her mind due to lack of sleep.

"What the heck has gotten into you lately?" her sister asked in frustration, throwing up her arms. "This isn't like you at all." Deandra agreed. She was not acting like herself, and she needed to leave now. She felt as though she was slowly being mentally derailed and as though she was being prevented by someone or something from meeting her basic human needs to function properly. Deandra begged her sister once more to come with her, and after she refused, Deandra left the Leland in tears, searching for a hotel to stay in until she could figure out what to do. Deandra ultimately decided to stay in Detroit and stick out the full three weeks with her sister but refused to go into the Leland after that. "Tension ran high the rest of that trip, and I could tell my sister was mad at me, but I just couldn't bring myself to stay in there another night after what had happened to me. Honestly, can you blame me?"

A long-term resident who identified himself as "Mr. Franklin" lived at the Leland years ago and was eventually moved out by family due to health reasons. Although he personally did not witness any paranormal activity while at the Leland, his health worsened so drastically while he was living there that he almost did not make it out alive. His neighbors, on the other hand, shared a story with him about something unsettling that happened in their apartment. A married couple had recently moved into the Leland, and every day the husband would leave for work in the morning and return home in the evening. One day when the husband walked into the apartment, he noticed a man sitting in one of the chairs in the living room. At first, the husband was surprised to see someone else in the apartment other than his wife. And then he felt a little angry. Why was there another man in his home, especially when he had been at work all day? Was his wife being unfaithful? Slowly and quietly shutting the door behind him, he turned to the man, saying sternly, "What are you doing in my home?" The man slowly turned to the husband, smiling, and gave a downward nod, not saying anything. Suddenly, there was a knock at the door, breaking the mounting tension. The husband quickly opened the door, just to see his wife standing outside it. "Hey honey, you locked me out. I thought I would make it back home before you got out of work," she said, setting down a large laundry basket and giving her husband a kiss on the cheek. He leaned back from her, suspiciously eyeing her up and down. "Who is this man?"

"What man?"

"That man, on the chair."

The husband motioned to the chair, only to discover that the man was no longer there. "There was just a man sitting here when I got home from work," he said, flustered. The couple looked all over the apartment and could not find any trace of a man having been there. Puzzled and a bit on edge, the husband did not know what to make of the occurrence.

Soon, it began happening sporadically throughout the day and night. The husband would get up for a drink of water in the middle of the night and see the man sitting on the chair in the living room, only to dissipate moments later. After about three months of this happening, the couple felt that the spirit was harmless and tried to ignore it to the best of their abilities, even though they were not exactly comfortable with the circumstances. Then one day, the couple was becoming intimate when they looked up and saw the man hovering over them. They both jumped up in holy terror, screaming and waving their arms over their heads. It was at that moment they decided the haunting had gone too far. They left the Leland with nothing but the shirts on their backs and never returned. Mr. Franklin confirmed that he never saw another man ever enter or exit their apartment during the short duration of their tenancy, and no one had ever moved back into the vacated apartment.

While ghost sightings have been reported all over the property, the very walls of the Leland ooze the despair, hopelessness and dysfunction that possesses the pores of fragmented souls. There is just something about the place that draws people in, captivates them and then slowly derails them. Now that you know its story, will the Leland inflict misfortune on your life too?

CAVIAR, CHAMPAGNE AND BOOS

My dear, our home is simply not befitting of your status," Flora Whitney lamented to her husband as she walked around scrutinizing her stately home on the corner of Woodward Avenue and Sproat Street. She and her husband, wealthy lumber baron David Whitney Jr., had the home built in 1870, and Flora envisioned a much swankier residence. "Anything for you, my love," he replied. David soon began planning to have the most lavish mansion in all of Detroit built for his beloved wife, although construction did not begin until 1890. Even though he personally was not an ostentatious or pretentious person, he wanted nothing more than to make his wife happy. If the house down the street had nineteen fireplaces, he knew Flora would want twenty. Flora's $400,000, sprawling twenty-two-thousand-square-foot Romanesque Revival dream home at 4421 Woodward Avenue, which would cost almost $10 million in today's money, would have only the best of everything. David had spent the equivalent of almost $14 million, also in today's money, on furnishings and art for the home. The home, which took four years to build, was completed in 1894 and included fifty-two expansive and extremely well-appointed rooms, Tiffany stained-glass windows, silk paintings, intricately detailed woodwork and vaulted ceilings, just to name a few of its impressive features. The home's exterior featured pink jasper shipped in from South Dakota, and it was the first residence in the city of Detroit to implement a personal elevator. A six-thousand-square-foot carriage house was built

View of David Whitney Jr. residence at Woodward and Sproat Streets, 1881. 443 Woodward Avenue, built in 1870. *Courtesy of the Burton Historical Collection, Detroit Public Library.*

behind the mansion. Regardless of the mansion and property's ethereal beauty, Flora Whitney died long before she ever stepped foot inside her modernized dream estate. Staff and visitors believe she resides at the home in spirit. However, Flora is not the only visitant that wanders the luxurious mansion in Midtown Detroit. The Whitney has developed a reputation for being Detroit's most haunted home and for good reason.

David Whitney Jr. was born into a well-to-do family on October 9, 1830, in Watertown, Massachusetts. When he was twenty-seven years old, he relocated to Detroit to become business partners with his brother, Charles. Upon moving, David managed two of their lumbering companies and expanded them from the eastern coast of the United States and Canada to the Midwest states of Michigan, Pennsylvania, Ohio and Indiana. For a period, the Whitney brothers operated the largest lumber trade in the entire country. In 1860, David married the love of his life, Flora McLaughlin, and together they had four children: Grace, David III, Flora Ann and Katherine. David was an extremely hard worker, and by the 1870s, he had purchased vast acres of prime forestland, began shipping lumber and iron ore to downstate Michigan from the Upper Peninsula and became an icon in real estate speculation. Because of his real estate dealings, he was referred to around the city as "Mr. Woodward Avenue." It did not take long for David to gain

Top: Flora Whitney. *Courtesy of Tony Muzzi of The Whitney.*

Bottom: The Whitney mansion, circa 1905. *Courtesy of Tony Muzzi of The Whitney.*

monumental wealth and success in the booming lumbering industry and become one of society's most upstanding citizens.

On February 7, 1882, David received the devastating news that his darling Flora had passed away at the age of fifty-one. He decided to continue with the plans of having architect Gordon W. Lloyd design the regal abode in her honor. Lloyd had designed other structures around Detroit, such as the University of Detroit's Dowling Hall, the Wright Kay Building and Central United Methodist Church, and David found his work to be worthy of Flora's wishes. As David was the wealthiest man in Detroit, money was of no concern. Only one year after Flora's passing, David married her much younger sister, Sara, so that the Whitney children could be tended to lovingly by a familiar face. David and Sara did not have any of their own children together. As the mansion was being built, Sara walked over daily to admire the grandiose estate. Once the mansion was completed, David, Sara and the four Whitney children moved in.

David was only able to enjoy living there for six short years, until he too passed away when he was seventy years old from a heart attack in the house on November 30, 1900. His wake took place on the first floor of the mansion, where his lifeless body lay on display for all to see. Joseph L. Hudson, the founder of Hudson's Department Store and close friend of Whitney, assisted in carrying his coffin from the home so that it could be taken to Woodmere Cemetery for burial. Sara continued living at the Whitney mansion until she passed away in the home in 1917 at seventy-three years old.

Left: David Whitney Jr. *Courtesy of Tony Muzzi of The Whitney.*

Right: The guest dining room on the second floor of the mansion was witness to many deaths. *Author photo.*

Shortly after her passing, the Wayne County Medical Society (WCMS) moved into the home, and a single caretaker lived there until 1932. The Whitney family were big supporters of the medical industry and wanted to do their part to help their community. The family did not require the WCMS to pay a down payment on the mansion before moving in and covered the annual fee of $15,000 in property taxes until the end of the Great Depression. Finally, in 1941, the Whitneys handed over the home to the WCMS, and the organization operated out of the home until 1956. For decades, the Whitney mansion served as a hospice for tuberculosis patients. Patients who entered the transitional stage of hospice would occupy what is now the guest dining room on the second floor of the mansion and would remain there until they passed away. In 1929, the Visiting Nurse Association (VNA) relocated its offices to the carriage house, and in 1957, they bought the property for $150,000 and spread more offices throughout the mansion. The association took care of the mansion until 1979 and then sold it to local businessman Richard Kughn, who saved the home from demolition.

After a $3 million restoration of the mansion, installing commercial kitchen machinery and preserving the mansion's historical integrity, Kughn opened a fine-dining restaurant called The Whitney in 1986. The third floor was turned into a bar called the Winter Garden. In 2007, Kughn sold the restaurant for over $2 million to former Chrysler public relations executive Bud Liebler. Liebler initially expressed interest in buying the carriage house, but Kughn refused, informing Liebler that he would only sell the carriage house along with the mansion. Liebler made some minor physical changes to the mansion, spent $300,000 to rejuvenate and restore the garden outside the home, revamped the menu and renamed the Winter Garden the Ghost Bar, because of all the stories of paranormal activity on the property over the years. In fact, in 2016, Liebler invited The Atlantic Paranormal Society (TAPS) of Syfy's *Ghost Hunters* to film an episode at The Whitney because of how active the place was. Other well-known paranormal TV shows also visited the site. While many spirits have been spotted over the years, it is believed that Flora is the resident spirit, as she is so emotionally distraught over her sister having lived in the house that was created for her that she is consumed by sorrow in death.

One diner believes she encountered the ghost of Flora in the third-floor lounge adjacent to the ladies' bathroom. The diner was enjoying an evening out at The Whitney when she felt the urge to visit the restroom. Upon entering the lounge, she noticed a woman in period clothing crying hysterically on the couch. "Excuse me, miss, are you all right?" the diner asked, trying to comfort the sobbing woman. The woman did not respond to the question; she just continued to cry even harder, her wails filled with a harrowing pain. Disturbed by how distressed the woman appeared to be in the lounge, the diner quickly found the manager and reported the incident. When management arrived at the lounge, the woman was gone. Hoping she was still in the restaurant so that they could ensure everything was ok, they watched security footage, hoping to find out where she went, but they never saw any woman leave the restroom from the time the diner reported the incident to the time they went up to investigate what was happening.

A woman sobbing is just a fraction of the ghostly activity that plagues The Whitney. Another lady who visited The Whitney on a slow weekday had just ordered a drink at the Ghost Bar when she paid a visit to the same lounge where the crying lady was spotted. Alex, the former bartender, had just finished making her drink and set it down where she had been sitting. After nearly an hour of the lady being gone, Alex began to worry as he saw her enter the bathroom by herself but not come out. Finally, when the woman returned to the bar, Alex gently approached her. "Sorry ma'am, I don't mean to pry, but is everything okay? I noticed you had stepped away from the bar for quite a while." The woman let out an embarrassed giggle as she took a sip of her whiskey.

"Oh, I was just having a conversation with your bathroom attendant."

"Bathroom attendant? I'm sorry, ma'am, we don't have bathroom attendants here."

"Well, I know who I was talking to," the lady said, taking another sip of her drink and sounding slightly irritated by Alex's doubt.

She began describing the bathroom attendant to Alex, further trying to prove that she was not lying. As the drink began setting in, the woman became more confrontational. "Look, I'll prove it to you. Come over to the door, she's in there right now." Alex made his way to the lounge door, peering in as the woman confidently pushed it open, expecting to see the attendant she was talking to. But no one was there.

Voicing her feelings of mistrust, the woman erupted, "This establishment is hiding people!" Alex, so confused by the outburst, got ahold of management to inform them about what had happened, and sure enough, when management watched the security tapes, no woman had entered or exited the bathroom door, except for the female customer who had been conversing with Alex. The bathroom attendant's identity remains an unsolved mystery. Various other apparitions, including a man in a tuxedo whom many believe to be Whitney himself, an elderly lady with a bun and a young girl in a tutu dancing, have all been reported by diners and staff alike. Cabinet drawers open unexpectedly, ghastly faces are seen in mirrors, whispered names are heard throughout the mansion, silverware gets rearranged and machinery

Front and side view of the home of David Whitney Jr., a three-story Romanesque-style home designed by Gordon W. Lloyd, located on Woodward and Canfield. Recorded in glass negative ledger: "D/Historic houses-Whitney, David." *Courtesy of the Burton Historical Collection, Detroit Public Library.*

operates by itself. One night when general manager Tony Muzzi was closing the restaurant by himself, he had his own paranormal experience that spooked him so badly he now refuses to be in the mansion alone.

All staff had gone home for the night, and he was making his rounds through the mansion locking all the doors. Just as he stepped out of the bathroom on the third floor, he heard a song being played on one of the pianos in the facility but could not determine where exactly the music was coming from. As Tony traversed the mansion's grand staircase trying to find the source of the music, he was overcome by a negative feeling. He made his way to each piano in the establishment, only to discover that no one was there and nothing was visibly out of the ordinary. When he got to the last piano on the first floor, the music subsided. Tony became so overwhelmed by the experience that he ran out of the mansion in a flash, not even bothering to turn out the lights. While almost every room in the home has witnessed paranormal activity, the third floor and the elevator are two of the most active areas. Staff often would see the elevator operating even during times when the mansion was closed to the public.

One such incident happened on Thanksgiving, when a father, mother and their little boy were visiting The Whitney for dinner. Hoping to ride the elevator to the upper floor instead of taking the stairs, the father pushed the button and waited for the door to open. When the door opened, he motioned to his child, "Go on son, step in." The child took a step backward and looked at his dad, confused. "Daddy, I can't go in!" "Why can't you? Mom and I will be following right behind you." The little boy shook his head. "No, daddy. There is no room for us. There are too many people in the elevator." The little boy's eyes widened as haggard individuals in period clothing filled the tiny elevator car. The parents exchanged a suspicious glance before scooping up their son and getting inside the elevator, much to the child's dismay. One can only imagine how traumatizing that elevator ride must have been for that little boy. After so many years of hearing stories such as this one, The Whitney's owners and management team desired to have paranormal investigators at the property to document these strange happenings on a regular basis.

The founding members of Haunt Investigators of Michigan always had an interest in the paranormal and were intrigued by Detroit's creepy legends. While on a paranormal investigation in Salem, Massachusetts, in 2012, they decided they wanted to make their paranormal team official and vowed that when they returned to Michigan, they would be looking for places to investigate around the Detroit area. Co-founders Marc Ortiz of Dearborn and Mark Waynick of Westland had previously visited The Whitney before starting their paranormal team and wanted to visit Liebler's Ghost Bar. After a fun night gambling at the MGM Grand casino, Marc Ortiz, Mark Waynick, Ed Kachadoorian and ten other guys piled into The Whitney at 10:00 p.m., excited to have a few drinks at the haunted bar. Upon reaching the third floor, Tony politely informed the men that the bar was currently closed and they would have to come back at a later time. Hoping to avoid disappointment, Mark pulled out a stack of big bills and flashed it in front of Tony's eyes. "$300 says you're open," Mark said, with a glint of excitement in his eyes. "Oh, all right!" Tony exclaimed as he began fixing cocktails for the crew. And thus, in that moment, a long-term friendship and professional business relationship was born. When Tony found out the men were paranormal investigators, he invited them to partake in a paranormal documentary project that was being filmed at The Whitney and was headed by a student from the Motion Picture Institute of Michigan. Then, a year after that, Tony invited the crew to host Halloween events at The Whitney, but the issue was that at that point in time, the team had never investigated The Whitney before and did not have any content to present to the public. After some negotiating, Tony finally agreed to let Haunt Investigators of Michigan perform their first paranormal investigation from midnight to six o'clock in the morning, followed by many, many more investigations as the years went on. Over the years, the public's interest in the paranormal also began to grow and eventually led to the team hosting two events monthly at the mansion. After spending many nights in The Whitney, the team was able to capture an abundance of paranormal evidence and confront the mansion's many specters.

The third floor most certainly did not disappoint when Haunt Investigators of Michigan came looking for ghosts. Ed was using a full spectrum camera when he captured a photograph of what appeared to be a man in a tuxedo with tails at one of the tables nearby the Ghost Bar, where many others have claimed to see the spirit of David Whitney Jr. Marc, on the other hand, captured an equally impressive photo in what used to be the absinthe room, a room off to the far right of the Ghost Bar. In the middle of the room used to be a circular green velvet recessed-arm settee, and a large oval mirror hung on the wall across from the outside window. As Marc stood facing the mirror, he took photo after photo until he caught an older man's reflection. Marc could clearly make out from the photograph that the man had gray hair with a receding hairline, was wearing glasses and appeared to be floating behind Marc in the window.

Ed Kachadoorian (*left*) and Marc Ortiz (*right*) of Haunt Investigators of Michigan. *Author photo.*

Marc also believes this photograph to be evidence of David Whitney Jr.'s spirit. For decades, customers sitting at the bar have caught a glimpse of an older man standing behind them in the bar's mirror. He has also been seen strolling the length of the bar at a leisurely pace until he reaches a set of curtains located between the stairwell and the ladies' restroom. He then evaporates into the curtains without causing so much as a rustle. The basement of the mansion is equally as active as the third floor, although it is not believed to be haunted by Whitney but rather his second wife, Sara.

The basement is used by restaurant staff and Haunt Investigators of Michigan for their monthly presentations. Upon descending into the basement and turning left, there is a hallway containing what is known as "the cage." The cage is a fenced-in storage area containing dishes, pots and pans, napkins and miscellaneous restaurant supplies. Often, when staff would come down to get specific items for special events, the storage area would be in disarray, as if someone had been rummaging through the items. There have been a handful of instances where supplies that had been locked in the cage were later discovered on upper floors. Eventually, essential

The carriage house behind The Whitney restaurant. *Courtesy of Marc Ortiz of Haunt Investigators of Michigan.*

supplies were relocated to other areas of the mansion to prevent this activity from happening. Sara had always been possessive over the home that she inherited from David's love of Flora and is committed to ensuring that all the household items are accounted for. While the fifty-two rooms of the mansion are teeming with spirits, the carriage house, which is eventually to become a wedding venue, is speculated to be even more haunted than the home itself.

While random children's voices are heard throughout the two-story structure, they are not believed to belong to any of the Whitney children, as by the time that the house was built and the family moved in, the children were young adults. The eldest Whitney child, Grace, began using the carriage house as her private oasis when she was thirty-two years old, and her spirit is believed to have never left. Up on the second level, in the back corner room, sits a small table just below a single window. This is where Grace used to sit and enjoy tea while watching the polo tournaments, which took place in the field just beyond the carriage house.

On Grace Whitney's death in 1938, the VNA packed up and sent away the last of the Whitneys' belongings, including the tea set that adorned the table where Grace used to sit. Immediately, the nurses noticed a change within the atmosphere of the building. Doors began slamming, sounds of women's heeled shoes striking the wooden floorboards echoed throughout the carriage house and medical papers would fly aggressively off desks. The

Removing Grace's tea set from the carriage house has resulted in increased amounts of paranormal activity. *Author photo.*

activity became so frightening that the nurses pleaded to have the tea set returned to its original location. Once the tea set was returned, the activity abated. However, it is advised to this day to never touch Grace's tea set, unless you want her wrath unleashed on you.

Deborah Fuller, a server at The Whitney, was stationed in the carriage house during the night of October 30, 2020, while doing a Halloween dinner event. During the night, a total of six tour groups came through. During a lull before the arrival of the next tour group, Deborah was sitting alone in the carriage house and asked the spirits, "Can you touch someone for me tonight so that I know you are real?"

About fifteen minutes later, a tour group entered the chalkboard room, and not even five minutes into the history of the carriage house, a gentleman interrupted Deborah. "I'm sorry to interrupt you, but do people get touched here?" Deborah glanced over at him, totally shocked. "Yes, sir. Usually, it is women who have those experiences, but yes, that is a common occurrence up here. What happened?"

"Someone just touched the back of my leg."

Laughing, Deborah verified that the man was stone cold sober. The tour then proceeded into the room containing the tea set and snaked back out into the chalkboard room. The same man from before began panicking and stated, "Something just grabbed my elbow."

Later, Marc Ortiz and Deborah met up with the same gentleman from the tour while he was having dessert. "Are you okay?" Deborah asked, concerned. He replied, "I don't believe in the paranormal. I came here for my wife because she loves spooky things. I am a former marine, and I do not startle easily at all. I am so freaked out because I don't know what to make of what happened to me in the carriage house, but one thing I am sure about is that I got touched." Who or what touched the man? Was it Grace Whitney? Was it a nurse or hospice patient? Or was it the imposing shadow figure that hides within the carriage house's darkest corners?

Marc and Ed from Haunt Investigators of Michigan encountered a hateful shadow person while in the chalkboard room on an investigation. He was witnessed once before by an individual on a ghost tour, hiding in the closet opposite Grace's tearoom. Then he was seen again, during a time

The long rectangular window in the center is where an eerie nurse has been spotted watching visitors coming and going to and from the mansion. *Author photo.*

when Marc was standing with his back against the door to the tearoom and heard a cross-sounding disembodied voice just before the door behind him abruptly slammed into the frame and then bounced back. Marc and Ed tried to debunk the door incident but were unable to replicate the speed and power of the slamming door. However, they had no explanation for the intimidating shadow figure that crept toward Marc and then disappeared into thin air.

Ed Kachadoorian revealing a safe behind a hidden door within the wall in one of the first-floor dining rooms. *Author photo.*

The final spirit to have manifested inside the carriage house is that of a sinister nurse who watches the cars drive into the valet parking lot in the front of the building through her sunken, hollowed-out eyes. She can be seen from the windows on the second story. Always watching and waiting, perhaps for an absolution that will never come. No one knows exactly who she is, but she has a way of instilling fear in people that do not expect to see her freakish, pallid face.

The Whitney is complete with hidden passageways, rich history and a myriad of paranormal entities; you do not have to visit a Disney park to experience a real-life haunted mansion. The Whitney's many ghosts welcome all foolish mortals. Are you brave enough to order your entrée with a side of boos? When leaving the parking lot, do not forget to wave goodbye to the nurse who seems to be peering into your very soul as you drive off into the night.

DESCENT INTO MADNESS

Approximately sixteen miles west of Detroit's bustling downtown area is the city of Westland, Michigan. With a population of just over eighty-four thousand, Westland is no small town. But even bigger than the city itself is the notoriety of the Eloise Asylum. While the complex included a poorhouse, farm, infirmary, general hospital, tuberculosis sanitarium, pest house for smallpox and psychiatric hospital, the history of the psychiatric hospital propelled "Eloise" into the limelight among paranormal enthusiasts and investigators, urban explorers and thrill seekers all over the world. It is believed to still be the home to legions of restless and discontented souls. After all, people were dropped off there and forgotten about at an alarming rate. For example, if a husband were sick of his wife in the nineteenth century, it was standard practice that he could easily drop her off at the asylum with few questions asked, and her fate would be determined by those in charge. Eloise gained infamy for its deplorable maltreatment of both those with mental illness and those perceived as such. Today, the D Building, also known as the Kay Beard Building, at 30712 Michigan Avenue is one of a few buildings remaining from a total of seventy-eight structures that were built on the property. It is also the only one accessible to the public. While it is reportedly haunted, the property itself holds a mystifying energy.

Over the years, Eloise was known by many names, such as the Wayne County House, Wayne County Asylum and Wayne County Poorhouse, just to name a few. However, on July 20, 1894, a post office was founded on the complex's property and given the name "Eloise" after Detroit postmaster

The Kay Beard Building, also known as D Building, is one of the last remaining buildings still standing on the property today. *Author photo.*

Freeman B. Dickerson's adorable four-year-old daughter. Eloise Dickerson Davock grew up to live a long, happy and fulfilling life, eventually dying at the ripe old age of ninety-three in 1982. Even though the name was implemented to categorize and differentiate the various buildings on the property, it left a lasting impression, and the railroad station on the property also adopted the name. Soon the whole complex started being referred to as simply "Eloise," and the name became board official until 1945, when it was changed to Wayne County General Hospital and Infirmary at Eloise. But the origins of Eloise did not begin in Westland; they began in Hamtramck Township.

In 1832, the first Wayne County Poorhouse was established in a crumbling structure at the Leib farm on Gratiot Avenue and Mt. Elliott Street. The building was in horrendous shape, and after the 1834 cholera epidemic struck the Detroit area, leaving dozens of children parentless, room became severely limited. By 1837, the poorhouse was overcrowded for its size. However, purchasing more land to erect another structure proved to be far too expensive within the city limits, so the county looked at purchasing land in the country. The county eventually settled on purchasing 160 acres of land for $800 from Samuel and Nancy Torbert in Nankin Township, which is now known as Westland.

The land included the Black Horse Tavern, which was owned and operated by the Torbert family and was a stagecoach stop for travelers between Detroit and Chicago who sought a warm meal and a good night's rest. The tavern was not considered anything fancy, as it was just two basic log cabins that were connected by a breezeway, but it was purchased with the goal of using it as the keeper's house. Keepers during this era were generally just ordinary people, such as farmers, who were looking to break into politics and desired a higher position of authority in society. The county then purchased another 120 acres of land so

Eloise Dickerson. *Courtesy of Tyler Moll of the Wayne Historical Museum.*

that it could erect a two-story wooden house-like structure directly behind the tavern for the residents.

In April 1839, 35 people were relocated to the new structure in Nankin Township; 111 residents at the poorhouse in Hamtramck Township chose to stay behind, fearing that the new poorhouse was located too far into what they had labeled as the "awful wilderness." Back in those days, it took a total of two days to travel by stagecoach between the two cities, and that deeply concerned a lot of people. Four years later, in 1843, the county sold the log cabin for only two dollars, and it was relocated to a different property. The county then built a sturdier brick building over the site, where the log cabin used to sit, in 1845. The basement of the new brick building implemented two cells that would be used for intoxicated and out-of-control individuals. Additionally, chains were affixed to the walls of the basement for people who demonstrated unruly behavior and were thought to be mentally deranged. Mental patients were thought to be less than human and were briefly housed with farm animals. Visitors and neighbors often were alarmed when hearing humans frantically screaming and crying in areas where animals were also kept.

In 1856, the brick structure was expanded, and two years after that, the wooden building was demolished. A large home for the keeper was built on

View of the Eloise Asylum in Westland, Michigan, circa 1916. *Courtesy of the Burton Historical Collection, Detroit Public Library.*

the front of the property in 1865 so that the keeper could better supervise residents living on-site. It was used by the keeper, his wife, and several attendants of the poorhouse. The number of people believed to be insane began growing over the next two years, and the brick structure was not only becoming unsanitary and crowded but also causing mental anguish to those who were sane. The problem was that the county had no way of officially determining who was of sound mind and who was mentally disturbed, as no doctors were consulted or present on-site. The elderly, the mentally ill, the rational, orphans, babies, the mentally challenged, the blind and the poor were all housed together.

In that era, people were separated only by sex. In 1868, an asylum strictly for those with mental illness was eventually opened on the property, but it was anything but a sanctuary. Individuals would be left to die after being chained to the walls or thrown in darkened confinement cells alone. From 1839 through 1881, various doctors from Detroit and Wayne rotated throughout the facility once or twice weekly and therefore were not able to keep up with any patient progress consistently. Finally, however, in 1881, a rule was enforced by supervisory staff that keepers were required to obtain a medical degree. Medical innovator Dr. E.O. Bennett was the first doctor to serve as keeper of the property and genuinely cared about the mentally ill, discontinuing the use of chains and isolation cells. He was believed to have cured many patients through various experimental methods of treatment. However, other doctors that visited the site were not as considerate to the patients, performing painful and personality-altering lobotomies.

Six years later, various other buildings began popping up on the property and were labeled in an alphabetized fashion, starting with A Building, which served as the administration building, then B Building and branching out accordingly. Many of the buildings housed wards for further separation of the mentally ill from the general population.

Over the years, buildings were torn down, and new ones were erected all the time, but the new buildings generally retained their original names. The Eloise community became self-sufficient with its own bakery, chapel, post office, police and fire departments, laundry services, railroad station, gas plant (which later became the electric light plant) and various other community-based establishments catering to human necessities and desires. Some 20 percent of employees lived on-site in low-income housing and even created and raised families there.

Between 1921 and 1929, due to a massive increase in the populations of Dearborn and Wayne, five buildings were constructed on the property at

Very few buildings remain on the Eloise complex today. *Author photo.*

the corner of Michigan Avenue and Merriman Road to house the mentally ill. They were buildings I, J, K, L and M. Medications for mental illness were relatively new on the market at this time, and unpleasant experimental treatments were often used on patients, such as insulin shock therapy, in which patients were injected with increasingly high doses of insulin to induce comas, and electroshock therapy, which sent an electric current through the brain and triggered convulsive seizures.

By the onset of the Great Depression, a 382,000-square-foot building on the property called N Building became packed with over 2,000 poverty-stricken individuals who got little more space than a bed and chair during their stay at Eloise. In 1931, one of the poorhouse buildings was vacated and underwent construction to become the first general hospital on the property that was open to the public, university students and pharmaceutical companies to test drugs. This same year, A Building was demolished, and Eloise's administration took over the lower portion of D Building and used the upper floors for mental wards. Fast-forward two years later to 1933, and a whopping 7,441 people were occupying the poorhouse, while an additional 2,600 people were added to the already crowded psychiatric wards. Over 100 ladies had to share just a handful of toilets. And you thought sharing a bathroom with the members of your household was bad! This busy time in Eloise history was known as the "boom years," and reports of patient cruelty became rampant.

Patients lived in filthy conditions, were mistreated by orderlies and received unnecessary treatments so that they would maintain a calm and comatose state. Omar Weiss, one of the patients at the facility, is believed to have been beaten to death just twenty-four hours after arriving at Eloise. Hospital staff claimed that Omar suffered a stomach ailment and obtained bruising on his body from being strapped down. Based on Dr. Anthony Abruzzo stating that the patient arrived without marks on his body and the condition in which his deceased body was found, the claims from hospital staff are suspect at best.

In addition to volatile staff, violent patients were being added to the mix. Mrs. Meggson, who lived one mile away from Eloise, was attacked with a jackknife by her own son, Rolla Spears, who would undergo occasional psychotic episodes. He carved her face with his knife and stabbed her repeatedly all over her body. She was found in the morning, clinging to life, and was sent to the general hospital, where she passed away. Her blood-covered son was found wandering aimlessly in the woods and promptly committed to the asylum.

As the Health Insurance Portability and Accountability Act (HIPAA) was not in existence, patients' names, diagnoses and details about their mental

Wayne County General Hospital and Infirmary nursing staff, 1951–52. *Courtesy of Tyler Moll of the Wayne Historical Museum.*

health state or deviant actions were printed publicly in newspapers for all to see. Even a twelve-year-old child, Clara Wotzke, was labeled as "idiotic and uncontrollable" in the local news, and her committal to the Wayne County Insane Asylum made headlines. The gut-churning stories of Omar Weiss and Mrs. Meggson were printed as well. Suicides were a routine occurrence among patients. Graphic details of suicides on the property were also printed. Jacob Beyer attempted suicide twice before succeeding on his third attempt at taking his own life. He leapt over a third-floor banister at the asylum, falling forty feet before cracking his skull open on the hardwood floor below. His first few suicide attempts were at the county jail, where his trial for burglary was pending. Another man, John King, who was just forty-five years old, also leapt three floors to his death out a window at the asylum and died from internal injuries.

Between the 1940s and the 1960s, Eloise was at its peak of overcrowding. State hospitals refused to take in patients, and because of this, patients underwent even more disturbing treatments and abuse at the hands of medical authorities. They were strapped down and spun in chairs continuously, immobilized by straitjackets, subjected to forced purging, coerced into baths that were filled with ice cubes or scalding water, had water injected intravenously by painful needles and underwent lobotomies. Upon the hospital's closure, vials containing brain matter from lobotomies were found inside the adjoining rooms of the sprawling complex's underground tunnel system. By 1966, with the release of Medicare, many requirements were imposed on the complex, and financing for state patients ceased. Patients of the state were released into the community with an emphasis on home care, and only private patients remained, reducing the overcrowding situations. The abundance of buildings was no longer necessary, and they were torn down. Almost four hundred positions were eliminated, as they were no longer needed. In 1974, a new mental health facility abiding by state Medicare rules opened. Eloise was no longer being state-funded by 1977, and because of that, on December 1, 1979, the state mental hospital at Eloise was closed after almost 150 years in operation. The new psychiatric facility was then purchased by the State of Michigan, and most of the Eloise complex was razed when the general hospital shuttered in 1984. It now sits as a shadow of its former self. Appallingly, over seven thousand patients were interred at the Eloise cemetery, with no other identifying grave markers other than a number. Considering the varying levels of abuse and archaic medical procedures that patients endured, it is no wonder that claims of hauntings permeate the property.

In the early 2000s, a former Eloise nurse was heading home after running errands when she decided to go see what had become of the former complex, as she had not been by there in quite a while. As she began pulling up to the building, she spotted an elderly, emaciated-looking man with wild gray hair in a hospital gown. He was bellicosely punching his right fist into his left palm, stomping through the grass and carrying on what appeared to be a one-sided conversation near the Kay Beard Building. Pulling into the parking lot, the woman rolled down her window to better observe his aberrant demeanor. After watching the man for a few minutes, she debated calling the police, as she had determined that the man was alone and seemed delirious. As the man turned toward her car, she let out a gasp of horror. *Could it be?* she thought. She immediately recognized the face of this man; he had been one of her most violent patients at Eloise decades ago. Shaking uncontrollably in fear after remembering the day of his death, she rolled up her car window, locked her car doors and began reciting the Hail Mary. As much as she wanted to just drive off, she sat frozen in disbelief at what she was seeing and could not bring herself to look away. The man's eyes locked with hers, and he began slowly approaching her vehicle. The closer he got, she noticed what appeared to be blood spilling from the corners of his mouth. Emotionally fraught, she tried to start her ignition, but when it would not fire, she glanced down for a split second to see what the problem was with her car. Fiddling with her keys, she watched in trepidation as the man stepped in front of her hood. *Come on, car, start! Oh my God. Please start!* the lady screamed repeatedly. Finally, after multiple attempts at reinserting her keys and turning them over in the ignition, her car roared to life. After looking down to insert her car keys for the last time, she glanced up, and the man was gone. *Where is he?!* Affrighted, she threw the car in reverse and sped out of the parking lot, with no plans to ever return to the property again. She seldom shares her story for fear of judgement and retaliation. The nurse felt that this patient had appeared to her because, at the time of his death, she was inwardly joyous that she no longer had to deal with his foul mouth and venomous anger.

Around the same time that this elderly man was seen, the lower two floors of the Kay Beard Building were occupied by Wayne County administrative staff who were also witnessing strange figures throughout the building. While they experienced the bulk of activity on the presumedly empty mental wards on the upper floors, coming to work in a haunted building was not without surprises.

One county staff member, whose office was on the first floor of the building, came forward to the local media about a regular paranormal encounter she had nearby her office with a female apparition. She told channel 4 WDTV newscaster Paula Tutman, "She's got light brown hair, parted down the middle. Kind of like a, you know, '60s look with the long stringy hair. She is usually leaning up against the window, just kind of staring out blankly." Paula asked the employee if she had seen other figures, and while the employee said she felt other presences, she told the reporter that the girl against the window was the only one who had clearly manifested.

Owner John Hambrick, who obtained the building in 2018, began allowing paranormal tours and overnight ghost hunts for the public. People from all over the world have come to pay their respects to the lost souls confined to the property and to try to communicate with those who have not yet crossed over. Detroit Paranormal Expeditions (DPX) was the first team that John contacted to head paranormal investigations of the historic Kay Beard Building. On August 31, 2018, DPX did their first walkthrough of Eloise, broadcasting it live on social media. About thirteen minutes into the video, an elderly lady can be heard on the third floor, whispering "What is that?" This was not heard at the time of the recording, so it was ignored by Jeff Adkins, who was filming, and his crew. However, only a few seconds later the voice angrily repeats the same question. According to DPX, they thought the older woman might be inquiring about the cellphone that they were using to film the walkthrough.

That same night during their investigation, Jeff Adkins was alone on the third floor. Each ward was pretty much laid out the same way with a day room, ward room and bathroom all opposite each other. To the far right side on the west portion of the building were showers adjacent to a linen closet, and across from that, on the east portion, was a short hallway with a laundry chute that led to a tub room. The tub room normally was accessible to the ward room, but on this night, the door was bolted shut, so there was only one access point into the tub room. A digital video recorder (DVR) system was set up in the west ward room, and cameras were placed throughout the floor. Around 8:30 p.m., Jeff began heading down the main hallway of the ward toward the right stairwell when he heard the disembodied voice of a woman loudly babbling, but he could not make out any distinguishable words. Initially thinking that the sound may have been coming from the right stairwell, he headed over to it, only to realize that the sound was coming from the tub room instead. Jeff turned around and stood facing the hallway as he called out, "Hello!" With the babbling continuing, Jeff walked down the darkened corridor into the tub room and made the discovery that he was completely alone—no woman was in sight.

At approximately 1:40 the following morning, everyone went outside to take a break, except for Todd Bonner, who was on the third floor in the west ward room making sure all the equipment was running smoothly. When Todd looked up from what he was doing, it appeared that he was alone. Suddenly, he began hearing shuffling in the back of the ward room. The shuffling then turned into human-sounding footsteps that were inching closer and closer to him. Thinking the DPX crew was pranking him, he began shining his flashlight around the room, hoping to catch a glimpse of one of his crew members. It did not take long for Todd to realize that he was by himself on the ward when he heard thudding footsteps coming at him, but not a single soul could be seen. He raced down the right stairwell and down the steps of the main entrance of the building to locate his team and tell them what was going on. For the next five minutes, the DVR system captured various sounds—the swishing of shower curtains, drawers opening and people walking around—in a building that sat completely vacant.

When other local paranormal investigators visited the asylum, they also experienced a lot of activity.

Westland native Faith Gearns has visited the asylum several times to investigate. The first time she stepped foot into the Kay Beard Building, she was overcome by feelings of heaviness and sadness that were unrelenting. "I just wanted to cry, especially walking through the third floor. I almost broke down into tears up there. It was crazy." On her second visit, while Faith was walking down the ward on the second floor, she began to feel as if eyes were following her. It was at this moment that she had this overwhelming urge to turn around and snap a photograph down the hallway, opposite the direction in which she was walking. Upon examining the photograph, she saw there was a lengthy opaque figure leaning against the door of a former doctor's office staring back at her. At the time, no other investigators were in the section of the building that was being photographed. Be it morning, noon or night, the spirits of Eloise never sleep.

While Eloise is renowned among paranormal enthusiasts, if you visit, try to remember that many of these souls were extremely dangerous to themselves and others. Handle your interactions with them with care and respect. If you say or do the wrong thing, there is no telling what could happen. When it comes to seeking your own paranormal experience at the former medical complex, just be careful what you wish!

BEHIND THE VEIL

In popular culture, most haunted cemeteries are depicted as being dark, dreary and neglected, but the Historic Elmwood Cemetery is anything but that. The picturesque grounds are pristinely maintained and serve as a final resting place to many well-known and prominent figures of Detroit's upper echelon and Civil War veterans. The cemetery also pays homage to other notable American and Michigan heroes. The hilly landscape boasts a certified arboretum with over 1,400 trees of 91 different varieties, a historic creek and a tranquil pond with a fountain. But beyond the façade of the beautiful grounds of this historic state site lie deep secrets of bloodshed and betrayal. It all began with the creek and currently ends with a monument depicting a veiled lady.

Prior to the summer of 1763, the Seven Years' War between the French and Native Americans ended. A treaty was signed allowing the French to give the land they acquired around the Great Lakes back to the Native Americans. Soon after this treaty was signed, the French left and the British descended on the area, seeking to annihilate the Native Americans and take over the land for England. In May of that same year, Pontiac's Rebellion broke out, as the English had seized Fort Detroit and the Native Americans wanted that land back. Pontiac and the Native Americans were unsuccessful in getting back the land. Chief Pontiac organized a coalition of multiple tribes to set up camp along a large creek named Parent's Creek, which is located on the western side of the property where Elmwood Cemetery is currently located. The creek was named after Detroit's first brewer, Joseph

View of stone Gothic Revival gate leading to Elmwood Cemetery; man stands in front of arched entrance. Printed on front: "Entrance to Elmwood Cemetery, Detroit, Mich." *Courtesy of the Burton Historical Collection, Detroit Public Library.*

Parent. While camped at the creek, Pontiac was informed that a barrage of British soldiers was headed toward the creek to attack the Native Americans. When the British troops arrived near the encampment on July 31, 1763, they were ambushed. Captain Dalzell and 160 British soldiers were so brutally slaughtered that the creek ran red with their blood. Today the creek is known as Bloody Run Creek and has greatly diminished in size due to becoming a part of the underground sewer system. While no British soldiers are known to be buried within the cemetery as it stands today, random sightings of soldiers in red coats have been seen by visitors. These apparitions are briefly seen and usually appear heavily wounded or in great distress.

Eighty-three years after the Battle of Bloody Run, in the spring of 1846, Elmwood Cemetery was established when forty-two acres of land in Hamtramck Township was purchased from a farmer by the name of George Hunt for $1,850. Detroit's elite wanted to create a cemetery within the city's suburbs. Throughout the years, additional land was purchased to enlarge the cemetery, and it now encompasses eighty-six acres of land. The reason the plots are in such great condition is because the cemetery became a nonprofit in 1849 and an endowment fund was initiated in 1883 for lifelong maintenance and upkeep of the property. Although seeing apparitions of anguished, bloody soldiers is frightful, another entity on the

Left: View of Parent's Creek, a small tributary of the Detroit River, which became known as Bloody Run after the Battle of Bloody Run. *Courtesy of the Burton Historical Collection, Detroit Public Library.*

Below: Bloody Run Creek as it appears today. *Author photo.*

grounds is far more prominent and formidable than any soldier you are likely to see. This entity's grave marker is one of the most notable on the property but almost didn't make it to the cemetery and has been a source of dread ever since.

Joshua Whitney Waterman, a Yale law graduate, met Eliza Davenport, and they married on July 4, 1846, in the state of New York. Together they

Joshua W. Waterman residence, located at 50 Washington Avenue, 1881. Razed on October 29, 1915. *Courtesy of the Burton Historical Collection, Detroit Public Library.*

had four children: three sons and a daughter. Their family relocated to the city of Detroit, where Joshua pursued a career in mortgage lending and real estate. Allegedly, all was going well for the couple and their household of active children, until Eliza's sister, Fanny, began tending to the Watermans' household. What began as domestic assistance soon blossomed into a secret romance. Eliza unexpectedly passed away on December 29, 1865, at the devastatingly young age of thirty-eight. Although Joshua had an affair with his sister-in-law, he still had a deep love for Eliza and, upon learning of her death, was heartbroken. Following Eliza's death, Joshua married Fanny in 1869. He hired internationally known artist Randolph Rogers of Ann Arbor, Michigan, to design a memorial in Eliza's honor, hoping it would not only commemorate her life but also make up for his shortcomings as a philandering husband. The twelve-foot marble sculpture depicts a floating woman with a veil delicately flowing across her face. The monument was crafted and shipped from Rome, Italy, and was part of the cargo on a sinking ship near Spain. It took two years to recover the monument from the site of the shipwreck. On the sculpture's second voyage across the Hudson River, it fell off the ship and needed to be recovered again. The monument finally made it to Elmwood Cemetery but was knocked over and damaged in a storm in 1919. Many believe that those who gaze upon the monument are destined for eternal damnation.

The Veiled Lady monument has been a source of dread since its arrival at Elmwood Cemetery. *Author photo.*

A young married couple, the Wrights, were visiting a grave site at the cemetery on a crisp fall day in 1998 and decided to check out some of the other headstones. They came upon the Veiled Lady monument, and Stacy Wright commented on how beautiful it was, reaching out to run her fingers across the detailed bas relief. As they continued to meander around the cemetery looking at the various names and dates on the grave markers, Stacy began hearing the crunching of leaves and twigs behind her as if someone was following her every step. Stopping for a moment to see if the sound continued, she felt a light tickle on the back of her neck. Thinking it was a bug, she raised her hand to brush it away, but she did not feel anything there. A second later, it felt as if a finger had swept across her neck, and it instantly gave her goosebumps. Feeling highly uncomfortable, she turned to her husband and asked him if they could leave, relaying her experience. The couple got into their car and were heading toward the exit when Stacy slammed hard on the brakes and screamed. "What is going on?" her husband shouted.

"I saw her in the backseat!" Stacy choked her words out breathlessly.

"Who? You saw who?" Stacy's husband whisked around in the passenger seat and saw no one. "Babe, no one is there!"

"The woman with the veil on her face. I saw her in the rearview mirror!" Stacy stammered anxiously.

"What lady with the veil? Oh…you mean…the headstone? Alright, hun, let me drive. It has been a long day. Let us just get home, okay?"

Stacy closed her eyes and tried to calm herself down. "Would you like to go grab something to eat before we get home?" her husband asked. "No, thank you. I just want to go home," she uttered tearfully, still quivering from fear. For the rest of the drive home, Stacy sat silently peering out the window.

A few weeks after returning home, Stacy began having regular nightmares about her cemetery visit, always seeing the veiled figure prior to waking up. After multiple nightmares, the veil started slipping off from the side of the figure's face, revealing decomposed and peeling skin. These constant horrific nightmares led Stacy to stay awake throughout the night, resulting in severe exhaustion and delirium. She stopped showering, picked at her food and was unable to carry out normal daily tasks. There was one incident in which Stacy's husband went on a business trip, and she was home alone for a long weekend. Per the usual, she passed out from exhaustion on the couch and was awakened by a drastic drop in temperature. It did not initially alarm her, until she exhaled and saw the misty cloud of her breath. Fully opening her weary eyes, she glanced around the room, fixing her gaze on the silhouette of a female figure in white with a veil standing in front of the basement door adjacent to the living room. The figure's gnarled and decayed fingers hung limply against her tattered, lacy white dress. Her chin appeared to be resting on her chest, although her face could not be seen from behind the veil. Letting out a whimper, Stacy discreetly backed further into the couch. She was scared stiff, and the figure proceeded to slowly tilt her head in Stacy's direction. When Stacy let out a yelp, the entity transported from nearby the basement door to the couch in a matter of seconds. As the figure savagely lunged at Stacy, Stacy threw up her arms to cover her face and head, which left her with several lacerations on her arms. As Stacy began to cry, the figure turned away from her and walked straight through the basement door, leaving behind a sickening odor of rotting flesh that permeated the room. Following the incident, Stacy found staying at home extremely difficult. But whenever Stacy left her home, she would panic if she saw anyone dressed in white, as it reminded her of the veiled apparition.

After months of waking up to the putrid smell of rotting flesh, an inability to keep warm and discovering painful bloody claw marks that marred her pale complexion whenever she was home alone, Stacy finally reached a breaking point. She no longer felt safe in her own home, and she would not drive for fear of seeing the Veiled Lady in her rearview mirror. "I felt like a prisoner. I could not escape the chaos in my life, and every day was getting harder and harder for me. I was being watched and attacked on a regular basis and no one believed me." Stacy's emotional condition further deteriorated to the point where she was exhibiting erratic behavior. She felt as though she was being traumatized relentlessly by this figure, and her health continued to decline. This ultimately resulted in her losing her job, her marriage and her sanity. Eventually, she had a nervous breakdown and admitted herself into a mental health facility. Upon release several months later, she returned to her childhood home to live with her mother.

Living at home, Stacy often helped her mother with her garden, and she immensely enjoyed it because it took her mind off things—at least for a little while. She loved that she had a focal point other than her trauma and found it healing. One evening after a full day of gardening, both ladies were tired and not up to cooking, so her mother offered to order takeout and go pick it up. Stacy was invited to come along for the ride, but she turned down the offer. She assured her mother that she would be fine and explained that she desired a nice hot shower to soothe her aching muscles from their productive day. Her mother understood, hugging her goodbye, and informed her that she would be back very soon. As soon as the front door closed, Stacy went straight to the bathroom to run herself a shower. She was relishing how great the steaming water felt as it cascaded down her sore body, when she heard a door close in the distance. Thinking it was her mom, Stacy called out,

"Geez, that did not take long, Mom!" But no response came. "Hey Mom?" Stacy called out inquisitively. Still there was no answer. From behind the semitranslucent shower curtain, Stacy could see a silhouette of a woman in white standing in the doorway to the bathroom. Stacy staggered back, frightened, as far as she could against the back wall of the shower and held her hand over her mouth to muffle the uncontrollable sobbing that came about without warning. Becoming extremely light-headed from hyperventilation, Stacy watched with glazed eyes as the white figure drew closer and closer. When the figure finally reached the shower curtain, only a thin piece of polyethylene vinyl acetate hung between Stacy and her worst nightmare. The figure's long and contorted fingers with dripping flesh came around the side of the curtain and grabbed hold of it. As Stacy lost her composure, her sobs pierced the once peaceful environment. As a defensive "Leave me the hell alone!" involuntarily escaped her lips, three light bulbs inside the bathroom's fixture shattered loudly into a million pieces. As the room went dark, it was filled with the malodorous scent of death. Instinctively, Stacy grabbed the rod holding the shower curtain and swung it through the air several times before eventually dropping to her knees and covering herself with the shower curtain as she wailed in complete and utter hysteria. Her mom returned home not long after, finding her daughter in an extremely vulnerable and fragile emotional state. Shards of glass from the light bulbs were scattered across the floor, making walking a hazard. That night, Stacy was in such a traumatized state that her mother distributed some sleeping medication to her, and the two women shared a bed, keeping the lights on the entire night. While Stacy's mother has never personally witnessed the figure, the ordeal continues to antagonize her daughter to this day.

Nowadays, Stacy finds even simple tasks like showering to be torturous. She said,

> *Even though I have moved, I still see her. Usually, she appears when I'm in a defenseless state, whether that be physically or emotionally. My life has been destroyed, and I credit that to no other than the monument of the Veiled Lady. There is something about that memorial that is truly evil. For your own safety, stay as far away as possible from that thing. Looking back, it is a wonder I am still alive to share my story.*

If you do catch yourself inside of Elmwood Cemetery, heed Stacy's warning to avoid touching the Veiled Lady's monument. You never know what type of energy may still be connected to the souls of the dearly

After touching the Veiled Lady monument, one Detroiter claims her life was destroyed. *Author photo.*

A present-day photograph of the entrance to Elmwood Cemetery. *Courtesy of Amy Shabluk.*

departed, so always use caution when interacting with any death marker. It is believed that Eliza's emotions from her husband's betrayal are being projected onto those who dare to interact with her in death. You may also want to request that the spirits not follow you home from the cemetery so you do not end up having to learn firsthand the horrors of this traumatic experience and subject your loved ones to the same pain and suffering that Stacy and her family went through.

TERROR ON WOODWARD AVENUE

Books flying off shelves seem to be a running theme at well-known haunted libraries. After all, the staff and visitors of the Sage Public Library in Bay City, Michigan, and the Willard Library in Evansville, Indiana, have encountered similar paranormal activity. Even the 1984 classic *Ghostbusters* features a scene in which the apparition of an elderly lady is floating and reading a book in a library. This sort of thing is interesting but not unheard of. But what if I told you that the reported paranormal happenings at the main branch of the Detroit Public Library are a cut above the rest when it comes to experiencing true paranormal terror? Although the current staff prefer to remain silent about the eerie occurrences within one of Michigan's most beautiful libraries, a former staff member has decided to reveal the truth about what really happens within the building when the lights go out.

While the institution of the Detroit Public Library dates to March 25, 1865, the main branch at 5201 Woodward Avenue was not opened until March 29, 1921. Various buildings within Detroit were used over the years to house the expanding collection of books and historical files until there was a need to erect an entirely new building to store the amassed materials. The white Italian Renaissance library with bronze doors was designed by Cass Gilbert, who is best known for designing the U.S. Supreme Court Building in Washington, D.C., and the Woolworth Building in New York City. From the enormous columns made of rosy Tennessee marble to the heavily ornamented ceiling, the front entrance has been compared to a

View of cars parked in front of Main Library, Detroit Public Library. Date April 9, 1929. *Courtesy of the Burton Historical Collection, Detroit Public Library.*

European palace. The library was created as a sanctuary of learning, and throughout the building's intricate interior are historic murals and art relating to classic literature, scholars and Roman mythology. With Detroit's population growth in the 1950s, the library expanded its collection to almost three million volumes. On June 23, 1963, wings were added on Cass Avenue to accommodate the additional materials, and the library doubled in size. One of the most significant aspects of the Detroit Public Library's main branch is that it houses the Burton Historical Collection, which is a collection consisting of a plethora of maps, rare unpublished and published works of literature, genealogical data and land records.

Local historiographer and attorney Clarence Monroe Burton began gathering documentation pertaining to the history of Detroit but soon realized that the documents included history of the state of Michigan, the Northwest region, Canada and New France. By 1915, Burton had obtained so much documentation relating to Detroit and the surrounding areas for his private collection that he decided to donate the accumulated files to the Detroit Public Library to aid in historical research.

Former Detroit Public Library employee Alejandra Amalia worked within the Burton Historical Collection for approximately two and a half years, starting her position there in 2007. Her work consisted of retrieving materials from the stacks of the collection for fellow librarians and individuals working on research projects. The collection was split up among the library's different levels. The top level contains documentation under lock and key, while other documents from the collection are stored in the basement and adjoining sub-basement. The sub-basement contains a climate-controlled vault that preserves financially valuable items, items of a delicate nature and historic photographs. It is a dimly lit area of the library with no overhead lighting, just lights that are affixed to each individual bookcase, with different switches at the end of each shelving unit. Multiple bookcases placed together form an aisle. For example, if a librarian were locating archived documents pertaining to the Whitney family and the files could be found among three bookshelves, the librarian would light up those three aisles, while the rest of the vault would remain pitch black. Alejandra described it as being "so dark down there that you could barely see your hand in front of your face."

While she admitted that employees always felt uncomfortable going down into the vault—basically a bomb shelter with nearly soundproof walls and poor lighting, where cellphones did not work—it provided the staff with a paycheck, so they tolerated it. One day, Alejandra's manager asked her to organize some files on a specific subject in the vault as they were out of place, so she headed down into the bowels of the library by herself to begin her time-consuming task.

When she entered the vault, she looked down each aisle to see what materials she could gather pertaining to the subject matter she was working on. In doing this, she walked between about six rows of bookcases, flicking on the light switches to each of them. The only sound cutting through the dead silence was the gentle buzzing of the fluorescent lighting. Alejandra began creating a pile of photographs that were needing to be digitized when she became overwhelmed by feelings of dread. She began sensing someone else was in the vault with her but decided to power through her feelings, chalking them up to the eerie stillness and darkness of the environment.

Stories of hauntings at the Detroit Public Library were regularly shared privately among employees, and Alejandra figured the tales were just getting to her. As she continued diligently working on sorting through the photographs, she tuned out the disconcerting feelings. A faint sound broke her concentration, and she gingerly set down the photograph in her hands, becoming hyperaware of her surroundings. Alejandra became totally unable to focus on her work. At the opposite end of the room from where she was standing, she could hear what she described as "a really fast pitter-patter, almost like a child was running." Forcing herself to check out the sound, she apprehensively peered beyond the bookshelf into the darkness as her heart raced with anxiety. At this point, she knew with certainty that she was no longer alone. Someone or something was down in the vault with her, but what? Or who? She felt her blood run cold at this realization.

Despite her fear, she tried to remain calm. Perhaps it was something as harmless as a mouse or another employee who had quietly snuck in there as to not disturb Alejandra and break her concentration. That was her thought, until she realized that she had the sole key to the vault with her. Even though she wanted to investigate the sound, she could not bring herself to venture away from the illuminated aisles. As her eyes scanned the room, the running sound finally ceased. Reluctantly, Alejandra returned to her work, hoping to finish sooner rather than later so she could get the hell out of the vault. As soon as she went back to what she was doing, the sound started up again. Once more, Alejandra walked to the end of the bookshelf to see if she could see anything, but nothing was there.

Becoming annoyed at the persistent interruptions and half questioning her sanity, Alejandra went back to her work, determined to ignore the disturbance. As soon as she reached for another file, she heard the sound *again*, this time much closer than it was before. As her eyes quickly darted to the end of the bookshelf, she saw something about two or three feet in height race by. "It was so fast; I couldn't make out what it was the first time I saw it. It was about the size of a toddler, and all I saw was just a small blur of red as it ran by." Alejandra felt her mouth run dry, her hands become clammy and her heart nearly implode inside of her. Trembling uncontrollably, she did not know what to do except stand frozen in shock, staring ahead and waiting for this odd figure to reappear. Sure enough, mere seconds passed before it ran past her again, this time heading in the opposite direction. "I know how crazy this sounds, but honestly, it looked like a gnome with a red pointed cap and outfit. I did not want to interact with it, and I did not know what to do. I could not do much of anything other than stand there petrified and barely able to breathe." Alejandra felt a surge of adrenaline rush through her body, and she bolted frantically to the exit, leaving her work assignment in the dust.

As time went on, Alejandra began wracking her brain trying to understand the sighting of the small red figure. "Being from Detroit, I've spent countless hours thinking that it was related to the Nain Rouge, or it *was* the Nain Rouge." Although Alejandra's paranormal encounter was an isolated incident, current staff members continue to avoid the vault for a multitude of reasons. Many people believe the documents within the Burton Historical Collection to have supernatural attachments and strange energies. Whether it be documents and books being rearranged by phantom hands or the harbinger of doom lurking in the Detroit Public Library's darkest corridors, the stories alone are frightening enough to deter even the bravest of souls from pursuing the truth for themselves.

SIT BACK, HERE COMES THE AXE

At the intersection of St. Aubin Street and Mack Avenue sits an empty plot of land where a home used to be until it was demolished in the mid-1940s. It is in a busy area of the city, so drivers are constantly going past, most not giving it so much as a second thought. However, on a warm and tranquil July morning, this plot of land stood witness to one of the most horrific axe murders and most outlandish true crime stories in the history of Detroit. To this day, the individual(s) responsible for the murders have not been brought to justice, and it continues to remain an unsolved mystery. The gruesome butchering of the Evangelist family has left a paranormal imprint on the area, and some passersby have claimed to see some disturbing apparitions wandering about the plot. While unusual and perturbing sights are pretty common in most big cities across the world, seeing a headless man walking nearby your vehicle in the dead of night certainly gives the peculiar happenings in places like New York City and London a run for their money. In addition, no one has dared to build another home on this lot since.

In 1885, Benjamino "Benny" Evangelista was born in Naples, Italy. In 1904, he relocated to America as a young man of only nineteen with his brother, Antonio. Shortly after arriving in the city of Philadelphia, Pennsylvania, Benjamino legally changed his name to Benny Evangelist and wisely invested money in real estate, which provided him with a great career as a realtor and landlord, enormous wealth and an impressive social status as a newcomer within the community. Always interested in the occult, he made

Author photo.

additional funds by selling black magic, herbs and remedies of a spiritual nature to vulnerable souls looking for help with their physical or mental ailments. His supplemental income included sometimes sacrificing animals or performing certain rituals with the intent to curse or cure others.

In 1906, Benny penned and self-published his own Bible after founding a cult, the Union Federation of America. He wrote *The Oldest History of the World Discovered by Occult Science in Detroit, Michigan* after undergoing trances each night in which he claimed God would reveal obscure and unknown information to him that the rest of the world did not yet know. He had intended to pen a total of four books containing these revelations. It was in this publication that he referred to himself as a "Divine Prophet," mystical healer and spiritual leader. His own brother, Antonio, a devout Catholic, disowned him after learning that he was experiencing these bizarre visions that went against Catholicism.

Benny left his cult and once again relocated to York, Pennsylvania, where he quickly found work constructing railroads. It was in York where Benny met his best friend, Aurelius Angelino. The duo discovered that they not only were both born in Naples, Italy, but also had a penchant for the occult.

The two men fell down the rabbit hole of the dark side of religion, and in 1919, Aurelius had become so consumed by the darkness that he assaulted his own family with an axe, brutally murdering two of his own children. The violent behavior landed Aurelius in an institution for the criminally insane.

Shocked by his friend's actions, Benny decided to migrate to Detroit, Michigan, where he pursued careers in both carpentry and real estate. Benny met and married his wife, Santina, and the two parented four children together. Their names were Angeline (eight), Matilda (five), Jay (three) and Morrio (eighteen months). Early newspaper reporting had originally identified the children as Angelina, Margaret, Jeanne and Mario, but these names are believed to be incorrect, and Jay was accidentally misgendered as Jeanne. Although there is much conflicting information published on the Evangelist family, it is thought that Santina and Benny did not know each other very well before tying the knot and all the children were Santina's from a previous marriage. One of the children they parented together died prior to the couple relocating to their permanent residence, and his name is unknown. Extremely limited information can be found regarding the son who passed away.

Although he enjoyed his day jobs, Benny found himself drawn once again into the world of the occult. He began offering psychic healings to people for upward of ten dollars, which was the equivalent of two full days of work. Benny would don a wig and beard during these readings to appear wiser than he was. People began regarding him as Detroit's "Hex Man," and he also became known around the city as a religious extremist and cult leader. Although some people believed that he was "out there" and a scam artist, there were a number of people who strongly believed in his visions and followed him blindly. This new revenue stream allowed Benny to move himself and his family into a beautiful, spacious green-colored home complete with a wide-set porch and basement at the intersection of St. Aubin Street and Mack Avenue. The basement became Benny's personal escape into a world that was closer to hell than to heaven.

Benny used some of the space in the basement to create the "Great Celestial Planet Exhibition," which involved approximately a dozen grotesque handmade dolls made of wax that were hung from the ceiling to depict planets and a lit-up eye depicting the sun that sat in the center of the figurines. The eye display was made with the use of lumber, electrical wiring and papier-mâché. Anyone walking by the Evangelists' home could easily see this display through the window. Benny also used his basement as a "church," and he had encircled the room with hundreds of copies of his Bible, which he had nicknamed "the sun." He also displayed a crude altar, stored knives and various jars for rituals, concocted spells and potions, performed hexes and violently slaughtered countless numbers of innocent animals in an effort to oblige his god. As Benny delved deeper into religious fanaticism, he began gaining serious enemies, who accused him of financially exploiting and ripping off people who desperately needed help. Doubt regarding Benny's healing powers began circulating around the city, as people who had paid him to cure themselves or a loved one were realizing that his so-called cures were nothing but a sham.

The night of July 3, 1929, Benny was conducting business on his carpentry job when he contacted the watchman at a home that was soon to be razed. He informed the watchman that he had bought up all the lumber that could be salvaged from the home's demolition and had scheduled to have it collected and delivered straight to his home the following morning. Benny told the watchman that he would meet the delivery man at his home with the intent to intercept and pay for the wood that he had purchased. In the wee hours of the morning, after Benny and his family were fast asleep, someone broke into the Evangelist residence and hacked the whole family to death with an axe. At approximately 10:30 a.m. on the morning of July 4, Vincent Elias paid a visit to the Evangelist home to discuss matters involving real estate with Benny. The delivery man with the lumber was a no-show, and Vincent was the first person to become aware of the brutal murders. He promptly contacted the police department to come out to the property at once.

When law enforcement arrived on the scene and entered the home to investigate, it was an especially grisly and heart-wrenching sight. Officers found Benny sitting at his desk in the basement, his hands folded in prayer on his lap, with his severed head placed near his feet. Three large photographs in frames featuring a deceased child lying in a coffin were placed around Benny's head. This was a postmortem photograph of one of the Evangelist sons who had previously passed away. When the police went upstairs and checked out the family bedrooms, they found Santina, who had been bludgeoned to death in the head as she lay in her bed. Most disturbingly, at the time of the murder, she was holding her one-year-old baby son in her arms, and the infant's skull was completely crushed by brutal force. The three other Evangelist children were discovered in the room opposite their parents' bedroom, hacked almost beyond recognition. Much speculation about who committed the murders and why they did it ran rampant, but the investigation ultimately led to a dead end as far as finding the sadistic killer.

Other than some peculiar items belonging to Benny that were found in the Evangelist home, the only true evidence police discovered regarding the murders was a string of bloody footprints and a bloody fingerprint that matched Benny. This was not enough evidence to convict anyone. Police sought the opinions of community members like Dr. Alf E. Thomas, who was Benny's doctor, and Anthony Esperti, Benny's lawyer, to uncover more clues in the case. Dr. Thomas confessed to investigators that he believed Benny was totally insane. Esperti revealed that Benny had been sued multiple times for real estate dealings, but the lawyer did not believe any of the lawsuits to be the reason for such an atrocity. Examination of Benny's criminal history turned up only a single misdemeanor charge after he installed someone's plumbing incorrectly. Benny's neighbors did not want to get involved in the drama, so they mostly kept to themselves. The general consensus was that while they viewed Benny as outlandish, he was harmless. The community, mutually horrified and fascinated by the murders, gathered by the hundreds outside of the Evangelist home, watching the bodies be carried out. The funeral drew a massive crowd of more than three thousand. Police carefully eyed each attendee in hopes the killer would be present. Unfortunately, it led nowhere.

Over the course of the next few months, several hundred people were interrogated by police and people with mental health issues in the neighborhood were targeted and arrested, only to be later released. Police tried to motivate those with any leads about the murders to come forward by offering a monetary reward of $1,000. No one ever did. After the police came up empty-handed, different conspiracy theories began circulating. One of those theories was that Benny had a hand in slaughtering Aurelius Angelino's children. There was speculation about whether Benny had framed his friend and escaped to Detroit, only to be found and murdered the same way as the Angelino children were. Another theory was that after Aurelius fled the psychiatric institution in 1923, he went after Benny for abandoning him in Pennsylvania and becoming rich from the occult dealings that they practiced together, as they were suspected to be a part of the same cult. One of the most bizarre, yet plausible, theories was that Benny was actually Aurelius. After all, there is no documented proof of Aurelius Angelino ever existing. It was assumed that he relocated to Detroit and changed his identity to evade consequences, only for karma to eventually find him. Newspapers have reported incorrect information pertaining to the Evangelist family and murders over the years, Benny's bible has been picked apart for answers, and the story of what really happened has continued to evolve through the passing years. However, the axe murders of the Evangelist family started a series of strange cult killings in Detroit from the years 1929 to 1932. The killer was never found in any of those murders either. While the neighborhood looks drastically different now than it did at the time of the murders, the dark energy remains, most of it appearing to be residual in nature.

Bloodcurdling shrieks and cries for help have plagued the remaining neighborhood for decades. Families lie in their beds sound asleep, just to be awakened by the pained cries of individuals being hacked to death through their cracked windows. Usually, it happens between sundown and the wee hours of the morning, around the time the Evangelist family was murdered. Some neighbors even claim to hear small children crying and begging for their lives, which they admit has been deeply disturbing to hear. But worst of all is the macabre sight of a decapitated man wandering the perimeter of where the home once stood before vanishing into thin air.

This supernatural phenomenon has been witnessed by multiple neighbors and vehicle traffic. The beheaded apparition appears downtrodden, with slumped shoulders and arms that hang limply at his sides. As he circles the empty lot, he moves as if stuck in a time loop, never approaching cars, homes or people walking. Many individuals did a double take to confirm that he was indeed missing his head. When people did finally realize they were looking at the sight of a beheaded person, they experienced feelings of abject fear, hysteria and shock, especially when the figure dissipated into the darkness of the night. The appearance of this man assumed to be Benny has also caused many close calls on the road with drivers. What would you do if you were driving at night and saw a beheaded man walking? Most people have fled in fear, but others have chosen to treat this ghastly sighting as a personal challenge to uncover the truth about the afterlife. Local paranormal teams and investigators have visited the area to try to witness and/or debunk the headless man phenomenon for themselves. For neighbors who have lived in the area for extended periods of time, the sightings are customary but still chilling.

Could Benny's dark dealings in life as Detroit's "Hex Man" have compromised the property that he lived on? Could the occult rituals that Benny performed in the basement of his home be the reason for this barren land? And lastly, could the many tortured animals that died at Benny's hand be also wandering the land in death, contributing to the cries that neighbors hear? These are questions that we may never have the answers to in our lifetimes. However, it is strange that since the killings, most of the original neighborhood has been dispersed and a lot of the homes have been removed

The Evangelist home used to occupy this empty lot. No one has dared to build on the lot since the family was brutally slaughtered in the home in the summer of 1929. *Author photo.*

due to urban blight. Could the downfall of the area be due to the downfall of Benny Evangelist? Let us hope it is just coincidental.

The next time you drive past this empty lot, remember what happened there in the summer of 1929. While this area of Detroit is not exactly a tourist hot spot, the area's dark past makes for an exciting and eerie jaunt for paranormal enthusiasts. Although there is no longer a home to see and the area is somewhat desolate, a visit down St. Aubin Street may bring you one step closer to encountering the headless ghost of Benny Evangelist, filling a void in your paranormal repertoire. Come witness the original site of one of the most brutal axe murders in Detroit's history and uncover the truth about the associated legends for yourself.

SOLDIERS OF THE SHADOWS

Since before Historic Fort Wayne's inception, tales of paranormal occurrences have endured at one of the city's oldest and most historic sites. The ground that Historic Fort Wayne sits on at 6325 Jefferson Avenue witnessed the first Nain Rouge sighting, a multitude of deaths over the last few centuries and supernatural phenomena as a result of the fort's dismal past. Encounters with the dead have been reported from all over the fort grounds. While combat never occurred at Historic Fort Wayne, the property and fort were used for various major events throughout history, such as the destruction and preservation of sacred Native American ground, colonization, the War of 1812, the Civil War, the 1918 influenza pandemic, World War I and II, the Korean War and Vietnam conflict and the 1967 Uprising. With so many historical ties, it is not a matter of if the grounds could talk, but when. Some have been fortunate enough to have encountered specters that may have experienced life on the fort's grounds, while others are still waiting for their opportunity to meet the spirits roaming the fort's ninety-six acres.

This location is currently owned by the City of Detroit and was added to the National Register of Historic Places on May 6, 1971. The fort grounds long served Native Americans for approximately one thousand years before ever being established as a military installation. The land remains significant to Native Americans, as two known Woodland burial mounds from the years AD 750 to 1150 existed directly on the property. An estimated nineteen

Platoon of soldiers stands in formation at Fort Wayne in Detroit, Michigan. *Courtesy of the Burton Historical Collection, Detroit Public Library.*

burial mounds in total had been built over hundreds of years within the Metro Detroit area alongside the Rouge and Detroit Rivers, but they have since been eradicated due to eroded land, theft, cultivation and the erection of buildings. Only one surviving burial mound exists within the fort today, and it is protected by the All Nations Veterans Council and the Historic Fort Wayne Coalition. The other burial mound, known as the central burial mound, was destroyed by the U.S. Army and the contractors it hired for the fort's construction between the years 1842 and 1845.

The origin of Historic Fort Wayne's ghost stories all began in 1701, when Antoine de la Mothe Cadillac and his crew of French explorers first set foot on Detroit soil. Driven by greed, Cadillac welcomed many Native Americans from the Potawatomi, Ottawa, Ojibwe, Wyandot and Miami tribes to relocate nearby the Detroit River so that they could become active participants in fur trade with the French. Nine years later, in 1710, the Potawatomi Native Americans were flourishing in their prosperous community on the land that is now occupied by Historic Fort Wayne. The land was the perfect place to set up a village with its proximity to bodies of plentiful fresh water and higher sandy grounds. The French called the land Bellefontaine, while the British referred to it as Springwells.

By 1760, the British had taken over Detroit based on a treaty ending the Seven Years' War. In 1780, the Potawatomi Native Americans sought permission to leave their village behind by writing a letter to Arent DePeyster, Detroit's British commander. They wrote a second letter stating that they wanted to leave their formerly used land and sacred burial mound under the care of Robert Navarre, a Frenchman who formerly held authority in Detroit.

In 1811, Michigan territory's governor, William Hull, sought assistance in Washington, D.C., for additional troops to fortify the city of Detroit. He was given the post of brigadier general and allowed additional troops but not provided with any navy men or ships. A year later, Congress declared war on England, and Hull took his troops into Canada. Sir Isaac Brock, a British general, responded by recruiting Native American allies to help defeat the Americans and seize the city of Detroit. Brock specifically called on Tecumseh, warrior chief of the Shawnee tribe, to unite allied tribes. Tecumseh had previously befriended the British and was renowned for enjoining different clans into a federation of tribes. While Hull was fighting in Canada, he learned Fort Mackinac on Mackinaw Island and Fort Dearborn in what would later become Chicago, Illinois, had been overtaken by the British and their Native American allies. He also learned that many of the American soldiers and civilians within the forts had been massacred. As an act of sabotage, the British commandeered a ship with supplies for the American troops. To further exasperate Hull, Chief Tecumseh and his fellow warriors hijacked a train containing essential goods, including food, for the American military.

Hull eventually surrendered, and the British overtook the city of Detroit, including Springwells, on August 16, 1812. The land was under British control for thirteen months. Hull ended up being court-martialed for cowardice, neglect of duty and behavior unbecoming of an officer. Hull avoided being charged with treason but was sentenced to death by firing squad. His life was spared by President James Madison, and Hull was given a dishonorable discharge from the army instead. While the army was unable to secure Detroit, the navy was building a flotilla in the state of Pennsylvania that would soon be victorious.

Commodore Oliver Hazard Perry, a Rhode Island native, is best known in history for his victory in the Battle of Lake Erie, reclaiming American soil and ending the conflict between England and America. The battle took place on September 10, 1813, when British ships attacked Perry's vessel, the USS *Lawrence*, resulting in the loss of most of the crew aboard. Perry abandoned the attacked ship and relocated his remaining men and himself to the USS *Niagara*. The British expected Perry to surrender after the loss of his ship, but he braved the harrowing conditions and went right back into battle, surprising the opposing navy. With a fleet of nine ships against the British navy's six, Perry was able to defeat the British and coerced them to vacate Detroit. Two years later, on September 8, 1815, the U.S. government met with representatives of all the Native American tribes that assisted as British allies during the War of 1812. The parties met at Springwells to sign a treaty that expunged their participation in the war, reinstated their rights and former possessions and provided the tribes with legal protection under the federal government. As a protective measure against further British invasion, the U.S. government implemented a plan to build a third fort in Detroit, the first one that was American built.

In 1842, the site of the new fort was purchased by Montgomery C. Meigs, the superintending engineer, but groundbreaking did not start until 1844. Meigs's first job was with Robert E. Lee, the future Confederate general. Together, they worked in surveying and became friends. Lee was sent to Mexico, while Meigs was assigned work on forts. When Meigs's son went to go fight in the Civil War as a Union soldier, he was killed by the Confederate army. Meigs blamed Robert E. Lee for the casualty and started Arlington National Cemetery on Lee's estate, his son resting on the property under grave marker no. 7. He also designed the arches at the entrance of the cemetery.

Historic Fort Wayne was established alongside the Detroit River and was less than half a mile from the Canadian shore. After eight years of building, the fort was completed in a five-point star design inspired by French designer Sébastien Vauban. It was then altered to better serve military purposes. A four-story limestone barracks building was erected on the grounds in 1848. A post headquarters, an officer's quarters, housing for commissioned and noncommissioned officers, a post theater, a jail, a brick hospital, a post office and various other structures, including civilian housing, were added on the property over time. The new garrison was called Fort Wayne after Anthony Wayne, a significant brigadier general in the Revolutionary War.

Fortification of the fort was not without casualties. As cannons were being loaded into their embrasures by groups of soldiers, a lone sentry by the name of William Pickett, no older than eighteen, stood guard in front of the massive leaden doors at the entrance of the fort. As the day went on, the soldiers hauling cannons became exhausted and fatigued by the laborious task they were performing. In error, one of the cannons slipped from their hands and hurtled downhill toward the heavy doors. The inexperienced sentry had his gaze fixed elsewhere and was unaware of the imminent threat barreling toward him. As the cannon collided with one of the doors, the door struck the young soldier with so much blunt force to his skull that it killed him instantaneously. Unfortunately, it would only be a matter of time until Historic Fort Wayne would witness innumerable deaths. After fortification, the fort sat idle with a single caretaker until it was used as an induction center for the Civil War, preparing Michigan troops to go into battle. To this day, visitors to the fort have reported seeing a soldier bearing arms at the fort's entrance. Perhaps the unlucky sentry is still trying to protect the fort, even in death. It is said offerings of whiskey and cigarettes keep his soul at peace. Of all the volunteers who make up the Historic Fort Wayne Coalition, Ed Kachadoorian would be most likely to know the truth behind the legends.

Ed, a paranormal investigator with Haunt Investigators of Michigan who serves on the coalition as a preservation specialist, has been a tour guide

View of entrance to Fort Wayne; group of soldiers stands in front of stone gate. Cannons decorate gateposts; soldiers' and officer's quarters are visible in background. Printed on front: "Main entrance to Fort Wayne, Detroit, Mich., 1301." *Courtesy of the Burton Historical Collection, Detroit Public Library.*

for many years at the property. Not only is Ed a true asset to the coalition, but he is also a walking encyclopedia of otherworldly happenings on the grounds, encountering entities from the days of Cadillac to the present day and everything in between. Through Ed's years of diligent volunteering and research, he has even brought some of history's darkest atrocities to light.

With Detroit being the last stop on the Underground Railroad, spirits of former slaves have been documented at the fort. Ed was with a group doing an EVP session in casemate no. 2 with an Ovilus-V, which is an Instrumental Trans Communication (ITC) device that converts readings from the environment into spoken words. In the darkness, Ed proceeded to ask questions aloud. Each response revealed more and more about the spirit's life and heartbreak. With the Ovilus-V, Ed was able to learn the story about a slave by the name of Isaac Cook, who was from Virginia. His wife had been sold off, and Isaac was unable to locate her through repeated attempts. After reluctantly giving up on finding her, Isaac decided to try to save himself by swimming across the Detroit River to Windsor, Ontario. Isaac never reached the border, drowning before he was ever able to claim his status as a free man. "That was a pretty intense evening. To get a first name and a last name out of a spirit is next to impossible and almost unheard of. It was the first and last time I ever got a full name while investigating!" Ed proclaimed excitedly. After the session, Ed decided to research the information he received. He discovered that the name Isaac Cook was a popular one during the early to mid-1860s, especially in the state of Virginia, so it was difficult to pinpoint historically who the man was. However, to date, Ed has found this experience to be one of the most surreal of his paranormal career. While the fort has many soldiers of the shadows, all seeming to represent different eras, sightings of Civil War soldiers of the Union army are the most prevalent. The soldiers of this specific time frame have been primarily spotted within the fort's different casemates, sometimes standing at attention and other times at ease, but always unaware that they are no longer among the living.

Another male member of the Historic Fort Wayne Coalition, who has chosen to remain anonymous, had an experience with a Civil War soldier that he would not soon forget. While volunteering one day, he was bent over inspecting the property near the powder magazine building when he suddenly felt a strong hand grip his buttocks and squeeze firmly. Startled, he jumped upright and whipped around, looking for the culprit. No one was there. After the initial occurrence, the volunteer found himself often being touched by unseen hands and had the sensation that he was being followed by someone

Group portrait of soldiers from the 2nd Regiment in front of a building at Fort Wayne, with trees in background. Handwritten on duplicate albumen print mat back: "Officers of 2nd Michigan Infty near Fort Wayne, Detroit, taken in May 1861. Folder 4, 6." Recorded in lantern slide ledger: "D/History-Civil War, Second Regiment, Fort Wayne." *Courtesy of the Burton Historical Collection, Detroit Public Library.*

or something that had a masculine presence. However, he was never able to determine who or what this entity was and why it attached itself to him. Then he heard the purported story of a homosexual Civil War soldier who was harshly tortured and viciously assassinated by his comrades because of his sexual orientation. His comrades promptly dug a shallow grave near the powder magazine, where his body was carelessly dumped and buried. The compassionless men covered their tracks just enough to evade consequences by their superiors. While the mistreatment, murder and death of the soldier was and still is extremely gut-wrenching, unjust and heart-rending, views about homosexuality were vastly different during that era than they are today. Soon everything made sense to the puzzled volunteer. While he no doubt felt sympathy for the deceased soldier's struggles in life, he also shared some nervous laughter with his fellow volunteers about the uninvited physical contact he received from what he assumed to be a very smitten soldier.

Twenty-two years after the Civil War ended, on July 11, 1887, Private Arthur Stone was also killed on the property. He had defamed an officer by accusing him of stealing an expensive bejeweled golden cane and was tossed into the fort's jail to await sentencing. Following a retreat ceremony in the afternoon, all the military prisoners were assembled outside, where an adjutant officer informed each soldier of the fate that awaited him for his crimes. A dishonorable discharge and two years of incarceration stared Stone in the face. As panic set in, his anxiety took over, and he attempted to flee the fort by running toward the fence that separated the military and civilian communities. Two soldiers unsuccessfully chased him, trying to get him to stop. "Halt! There's a load after you!" Despite the threat, Stone refused to stop running. Sergeant James Clark, who was inspecting the jail at this time, overheard commotion outside and came out to see what was going on. When Clark realized what was happening, he also warned Stone to stop running. When Stone did not, Clark quickly loaded his rifle and fired a .45-caliber bullet straight into Stone's back. Stone was taken back to his holding cell, where he died later that night. The ultimate twist in this story was that Clark and Stone were close friends, and Clark was unaware of the fallen soldier's identity at the time he shot him. Ed believes he has captured Stone's voice on his digital recorder. He was standing outside the drunk tank where Stone was kept, when upon playback of his recording device, he clearly heard a man say, "I'm in here!"

Another death that was recorded on-site was that of Elsie Wolwine. On April 11, 1908, Elsie, who was only twenty-two years old, ingested carbolic acid inside her bedroom in the Commandant's Building (108). Elsie had worked as a servant for Captain French and lived on the second floor in the back portion of the building where the servant quarters were located. Her death certificate indicated that she was married only a year before her death, had no children to call her own and was despondent during the time she worked at the fort. It is speculated that her husband had abandoned her, leaving her bereft. In October 2019, Ed was leading tour groups through the fort, and each time they passed by Building 108, a glow could be seen from the second-floor window. Since there was no

MRS. ELSIE WOLWINE.

The only known photograph to exist of Elsie Wolwine. *Courtesy of Phil Vermeulen of the Historic Fort Wayne Coalition.*

active electricity in the building, the groups tried to debunk the source of the glow but could not find a logical explanation for it. Ed remains mystified by the experience. "It looked as if a candle was flickering up there. I'm still trying to figure out what the heck it was." Fortunately, Ed has yet to encounter anything sinister on his tours at the fort. "I do not believe there to be anything evil here. I have gotten cursed at by spirits but have never been exposed to anything malevolent."

Investigators Jenny LaBay of Clarkston and Rick Frame of Howell cannot say the same. On two separate occasions, they encountered the fort's dark side.

Jenny has been labeled within the paranormal community as a "beacon of the dead." One fall evening, she was stationed on the first floor of the recreation hall adjacent to the bowling alley with another investigator. While there, the other investigator informed her that a hostile soldier occupied the modestly sized room that they were standing in. Apparently, this soldier was a bully in life and remained one in death. As Jenny's investigative partner turned out the lights, the room went black as coal. In the darkness, Jenny's other senses became heightened, and she felt a baleful presence enter the room. The figure stood facing her, ready for battle. As he began stomping toward her, she got into a fighting stance, unwilling to succumb to the negative entity. Without warning, the entity rushed her, but despite his intimidation tactics, Jenny refrained from moving. The bitter soul left her wrapped in a cloud of frozen air, as if she was stuck outside on a winter day. As she gasped from the chill, the lights flicked on, and the other investigator, aware that something alarming had occurred, hurried to Jenny's side to make sure she was okay. A visibly shaken Jenny was accompanied outside, where she deeply inhaled the fresh air to calm her nerves. Beneath the night sky, Jenny's friend explained that the belligerent soldier was not only a misogynist who really despised strong women but also enjoyed pushing people to their breaking points for sport. Because Jenny refused to back down, her encounter with this figure was a one-time ordeal. While this wasn't Jenny's only jarring encounter on the property, it is one that continues to linger in her memory all these years later.

Although Rick's experience was not as directly physical as Jenny's, it was equally as imperiling. During a public hunt, Rick desired to sneak off on his own and investigate the officer's quarters. Unfortunately, less seasoned investigators were also present that night, and one of them was trailing behind Rick, observing his techniques. With a needle-like focus on his investigation, Rick advanced down the hallways of the building with his Sony Handycam. At each doorway he passed, he would ask if anyone was inside. Finally reaching one of the last open doors on the left side of the hallway, he inquired once more if anyone was inside. As the door began slowly closing, doubt filled Rick's head. Thinking it was another investigator playing a joke on him, rolling his eyes, he began loudly verbalizing his annoyance. "Yeah, whatev..." Before Rick could get out the full word, the door slammed shut inches from his face. "After the door slammed shut, it then bounced off the jamb, eventually opening all the way in one swift motion, exposing the room in front of me. No one was in there." Both Rick and the woman walking behind him were startled, yet amazed, at the aggressive incident. Even though other investigators were in the same vicinity as the duo, no other investigators were in immediate sight of where the activity occurred. "I was over the moon with excitement and adrenaline. I could not believe it. But deep down, I always believed it. The video says it all. I could have quit the paranormal right then and there and would have been satisfied," he said.

Because Rick and Jenny were regulars of the paranormal hunts at the fort, they handled their spooky encounters with serious courage, but the same could not be said for everyone. An event in the summer of 2013 gave locals an opportunity to investigate the paranormal with cast members of the original *Ghost Hunters* on the Syfy channel. Steve Gonsalves and Dave Tango (best known simply as "Tango") of The Atlantic Paranormal Society (TAPS), two of the show's most popular television personalities, were present at the event. Tickets sold for $250 a person. After a lengthy meet-and-greet, the duo led a group of aspiring investigators into the headquarters building. The building had previously served as a Head Start school but was later closed due to not being compliant with the Americans with Disabilities Act. The investigation was underway on the first floor of the building, in the classroom directly across from the fort's research library. A dozen participants lined up against the wall of the classroom as they laughed and listened to the ongoing banter between Steve and Tango. Suddenly, the room gasped in shock and stared in horror as a dark shadow rose unexpectedly out of the center of the floor and hovered for several seconds before slowly melting away into the unknown. Two of the ladies participating let out bloodcurdling screams, grabbed each other in fright and scurried to the safety of the inside of their car. Their car tires spewed gravel as the driver sped out of the driveway, leaving Fort Wayne in a plume of dust. $500 gone forever.

The headquarters building is one of a few that Ed attributes as being one of the most haunted on the property. It was in that same classroom he had one of his own unnerving experiences. One evening, Ed was utilizing an SLS-XCam, a Structured Light Sensor device that allows users to access visual data that cannot be seen by the naked eye, often manifesting the data in stick figure format. Through the device, Ed picked up on a small figure about the size of a soda pop can that was running all over the room. At first, he wondered if it could have been a rodent or some other small animal but could not see the figure anywhere even after illuminating the room with his flashlight. Stranger yet, the figure had appeared on the SLS-XCam as a small black mass, similar to what the participants of the celebrity ghost hunt had witnessed. Finally, Ed cornered the roaming mass, and as he drew closer, the figure morphed into a headless human stick-figure. Apprehensive about the sudden change in shape, Ed decided to change his approach of contacting the figure and began asking questions. After a handful of seconds, the figure dematerialized.

Many paranormal investigators believe that the reason Historic Fort Wayne has such an abundance of ghostly sightings is due to the limestone used within structures on the property, including but not limited to the barracks. The fort's proximity to water has also been believed to be a contributing factor of mysterious happenings. Limestone and water have long been believed to be conduits of paranormal activity, as they are thought to increase the electromagnetic field and harbor spiritual energy. When one is subjected to elevated levels of electromagnetic energy, it can cause one to feel ill or disoriented, sometimes even resulting in hallucinations. There's an ongoing debate within the paranormal community on whether limestone and water really attract spirits and store their energies or if these occurrences are just a simple matter of being physically affected by environmental factors. In a 2011 interview with HuffPost, world-renowned paranormal researcher Jason Hawes of *Ghost Hunters* fame stated, "One thing we found is that you find more paranormal activity around flowing streams of water, railroad tracks and places with high limestone deposits." Regardless of what you personally believe, paranormal teams from near and far have credited the limestone structures as being hot spots of activity. Shortly before TAPS had their event at the fort, Brian Danhausen, founder of Into the Afterlife Paranormal and an empathic medium, had an otherworldly experience that appeared to validate Hawes's statement.

On May 4, 2013, a paranormal muster was taking place on the fort grounds, and hundreds of individuals gathered from all over the world to attend the event. Local paranormal teams, new age authors and haunted attractions were showcasing evidence and selling merchandise. At dusk, the Midwest's largest ghost hunt was to take place. Brian was one of the co-sponsors of the event, and each sponsor was to be assigned an area on the grounds to assist both new and seasoned paranormal investigators with perfecting their investigative techniques. Brian had requested to be stationed at the barracks building, as this is where he had experiences on previous visits to the fort. He would be demonstrating proper use of audio recorders during electronic voice phenomena (EVP) sessions so that investigators could get optimal evidence. While Brian was waiting for the next group to arrive, he was caught off guard when he spotted a young girl with braids in her hair. He slowly lowered himself to the floor to communicate with her in a nonthreatening way. When he got to the floor, he reached out his hand and invited the child to come closer. She approached him with her hand outstretched as if to say hello. When his hand intertwined with hers, he was overcome by a feeling of intense sadness that he could not explain. As the two sat in silence, it was as if time had stopped. The only other thing that Brian was aware of in that amazing moment was that his eyes were watering. The spiritual connection was soon disrupted when the next group of investigators entered the barracks building. Much to Brian's dismay, the child disappeared into thin air. That same evening, another investigator also captured the voice of a child on their digital recorder while Brian was present. Those who frequent the fort have also caught sight of a young girl peeking around the fort's many corners, both inside the buildings and outside on the grounds. Could this be the same child that Brian encountered? And if so, what reason would a child have to be on fort grounds in the first place?

Volunteers speculate that the female child fell victim to the 1918 influenza pandemic and has been trapped inside the fort ever since. The pandemic hit Detroit with a vengeance in January 1918 and lasted until December 1920. World War I intensified the spread of the virus due to military travel and large gatherings. During this time in history, the fort hospital was only one of a few within the city, and many civilians were sent there for treatment. Citizens who caught the illness were plagued by delirium, uncontrollable fever and profuse bleeding from the nose and the lungs. Sufferers even had their faces and lungs turn blue.

To try to control the spread of the virus, many of the same safety precautions of the recent COVID-19 pandemic were put in place. Nonessential businesses were closed; masks were being issued to citizens; and proper handwashing, social distancing and quarantining were heavily encouraged. Some individuals rejected advice from medical professionals and took it into their own hands to try to save themselves from the raging influenza. Some consumed turpentine and kerosene-laced sugar, and others rinsed their mouths with chlorinated soda and boric acid. Some even soaked in a hot bathtub full of diced onions with the hope that it would ward away the viral infection. Regardless of the lengths many people went to in order to prevent contracting the illness, an estimated total of 50 million people around the world lost their lives because of it. About 675,000 of the 50 million people who died were Americans. To break the statistics down even further, 3,814 Detroiters died as a result of the pandemic, and a considerable number of those lives lost in Detroit were within the garrison.

Today, Historic Fort Wayne serves as a community venue hosting festivals, weddings, meetings and markets as well as events for athletes, reenactors and veterans. Historical and paranormal walking tours are still offered on the property, even if the overnight ghost hunts are not. A visit to the fort is one of the best ways to support a valuable piece of American and Michigan history and possibly catch a glimpse of one of the fort's many specters. While you now know the story of historical figures like Private Arthur Stone and Elsie Wolwine, perhaps you will discover the truth about the fort's many other ghostly inhabitants on your next trip—like the mischievous elemental spirit that resides in the first casemate and loves to prank tourists or the early French settlers who just cannot wait to ask, "Parlez-vous Français?" These otherworldly beings have all claimed the fort as their eternal home and have no intent on leaving any time soon. So, be sure to stop by and say hi. They are waiting for you.

ILLUSIONS OF EVIL

In Greek mythology, Erebus was the primordial god of darkness, the son of Chaos and the brother of Nyx (night). The name Erebus also refers to the darkness beneath the Earth through which the dead must pass in order to reach Hades. In 1998, when the Terebus brothers, Jim and Ed, purchased the whopping 100,000-square-foot building that now houses their haunted attraction, they were seeking the perfect name for it. Upon hearing this, their father looked at them astounded and asked incredulously, "Are you both nuts?" After all, the Terebus brothers had been in the haunt business since 1981 before acquiring the massive location at 18 South Perry Street in downtown Pontiac, which is approximately thirty-one miles from Detroit by car. A name change was extremely risky after developing such a positive reputation for themselves in the region, but the brothers decided that a new building warranted a new name. Oddly enough, the brothers did not have to look much further than their own last name. One night while reading a vampire novel, Ed came across the name Erebus but didn't know what it represented. After doing some research online and speaking with Jim, the two decided that the name was a perfect fit for the type of haunted attraction they wanted to create. Thus, Erebus was born, and it most certainly lived up to its given name both from an entertainment and spiritual perspective. Unbeknownst to Jim and Ed, the building had a wickedness inside that lay dormant for many years. It was only a matter of time before it would reveal itself to the world.

Erebus is located at 18 South Perry Street in downtown Pontiac. *Author photo.*

The idea to work in such a unique industry came about when one of Jim's former employers made him join the United States Junior Chamber, also known as the Jaycees, which is a nonprofit organization that provides leadership training through community service. The year he joined was the year his group decided to put on a haunted house. Jim found his passion through his volunteer efforts but eventually left the job after being hired to work for Ford Motor Company. Unfortunately, he was laid off at just twenty-eight. When Jim was laid off, Ed was only eighteen, in the process of graduating high school, and he was undecided on what career path he wanted to take in life. Instead of sulking about his bad luck, Jim went back to his passion and decided to assemble a twelve-thousand-square-foot portable haunted house in his backyard. With Ed's help, Jim took the pop-up haunted house to the corner of Twelve Mile Road and Van Dyke Avenue in Warren. Admission was only $1.50, and at the end of the season, the brothers had a business loss of approximately $500. Thinking of ways to attract more customers so that they could profit from their endeavors, the duo decided they were going to apply to set up their haunt in front of the Kmart store in that area but thought it would be a long shot. To their delight, their cousin worked for the man in charge of those decisions, and he gave the Terebus brothers the go-ahead. While this move appeared to draw more attention from the public, the haunt had been set up on a low part of the parking lot, and every time it rained, customers would have to wade through four inches of water.

The man-made haunt proved to be no match for the accumulated rain, so the brothers decided to replace their pop-up haunt with mobile home trailers. They found trailers for sale that had been damaged by flames and smoke from flash fires. The damage was of little concern to the brothers, as they planned to do a gut renovation of the units anyways.

In just under two decades, the brothers had grown their mobile haunt known as the Haunted Gallery exponentially. They had become so successful that they upgraded their portable haunt from a reasonable twelve thousand square feet to an incredible ninety-eight thousand square feet of space. This enormous change resulted in setting up and tearing down ten fourteen-foot-wide by seventeen-foot-long mobile home trailers repeatedly. The trailers were so large that they took up two lanes of traffic, and Jim and Ed had to obtain special permits for them. Between paying to store, decorate and break down the trailers and the additional cost of water and electricity, it was no longer financially feasible to continue operating such a large and growing mobile business. After Ed sold his home and Jim remortgaged his, they finally had enough money to invest in their stationary haunt.

The building that now houses Erebus was vacant for forty years before the Terebus brothers purchased it. Jim and Ed located a permit within the building from 1928. In past years, the basement was used by a cab company, the ground floor was used for retail shops, the second floor housed a bar that featured a bowling alley and cue sports and the third floor was used for office space. A parking garage ran through the building, and the roof was used as its main lot. The structure was meant to be six stories instead of four, but when the Great Depression hit, the plan to expand ceased. Between 1930 through 1960, it was used as an indoor junkyard where old Cadillacs were scrapped.

Ed lived in the building when it was first purchased, and it remained his main residence until 2013. He often slept in different areas on-site before establishing living quarters on the third floor, which he still uses as his home away from home. Shortly after moving in, Ed began feeling that he was not alone in the building. "Since I was living there, I wanted to explain it all away." But some things cannot be explained.

When Ed would lie down for the night, he would hear noises all night long as if someone was in the building with him. Sounds of footsteps, banging, clanking and someone talking all penetrated the silence and made falling asleep extremely difficult. Occasionally, a hoarse male voice could be heard calling out for Ed repeatedly just beyond the wall of his third-floor loft. On two separate occasions, Ed was so convinced that someone had broken in, he ended up phoning the police department. After the police showed up with a K-9 unit and searched the premises, not a single living soul other than Ed was found on-site. After speaking with neighbors about the nightly commotion, Jim and Ed were told the rumor of a homeless man who had frozen to death and eventually turned to dust in the basement's boiler room. Wanting to explore the rumors, the duo descended the stairs to the basement and made their way to the cumbrous door of the boiler room. Upon opening the door, the brothers experienced overwhelming feelings of dread and despair. Trudging through debris of fallen bricks and other materials from the decaying building, they stumbled upon an old box of cereal along with a petrified red and green sweater, pillow and blanket in a corner of the room. Coal also sat nearby in a pile on the floor as haunting proof that the homeless man attempted to survive the harsh winter by building a fire but was tragically unsuccessful. Although the brothers promised to leave the discovered items alone out of respect for the deceased, discovering the homeless man's belongings stirred up a whirlwind of paranormal activity within the building, even darker than their wildest nightmares.

Steve Shipp, the art director at Erebus, began having his own experiences from the minute he stepped foot in the building in 1999. "It is really appealing for patrons to come visit us and experience a *haunted* haunted house, but it is a little different when you are a worker, and you are obligated every day to go to the *haunted* haunted house." Prior to Erebus opening in 2000 and Steve accepting a full-time position, he ran a fossil reproduction company out of what is currently the makeup room. After each workday, Steve and his wife would come to the building and work on fossil replicas for a few hours each night. The pair became accustomed to the sounds of the building, especially the distinct sounds of the metal doors as they were opened and closed. Like clockwork, when the couple were alone in the building, they could hear doors being slammed so loudly it was as if they were going to rip off their hinges. Steve would grab his flashlight and wander around looking for any sign of life but could never find anyone. When he began working for Erebus and spending even more time there, encountering the paranormal became

Abandoned belongings found in a corner of the boiler room inside Erebus. *Author photo.*

inevitable no matter how much he wanted to avoid it. He remembers the day he saw Erebus's inhuman entity for the first time as if it were yesterday.

Steve and his wife were in the basement by themselves painting walls and doing finish work when a domineering six-to-seven-foot opaque shadow figure quickly passed from right to left by the doorway of the room in which they were working. With no hesitation, Steve stuck his head out of the doorway to see where it was going, but it was nowhere to be found. Even though the figure could no longer be seen, it left both Steve and his wife in a cloud of dread and oppression. The figure continued to spread a sense of trepidation wherever he went.

Steve normally is the first to arrive in the building, starting his shift between 4:30 and 5:00 a.m. During those hours, it is still dark outside, and Steve often uses the flashlight feature on his phone to navigate his way to the first light switch within the building. Many times, during this process, Steve has heard what sounded like shuffling footsteps nearby. One morning when he heard the shuffling, he went to camera mode and started to document his experience, capturing what he perceived to be the same shadow figure from before quickly passing in front of him. It was only a matter of time before the nefarious figure would appear again to Steve, this time with an intent to cause serious harm.

His most sinister and frightening experience with the figure happened in February 2017, when the front lobby was in the process of being remodeled. Steve was working on the layout for the haunted house in the main office, as it was the only room that was heated. When he was asked to make a quick run into the lobby to measure something, he did not bother grabbing his coat or keys, as he figured he would only be gone for a couple minutes. Steve left the office, took a left down the hallway and entered through the doorway into the front lobby. While in the lobby, Steve began hearing strange, indistinct sounds coming from the propped-open door through which he had entered a few minutes prior. He grabbed the phone out of his pants pocket and opened his camera to snap a few quick photographs. While doing so, the open door slammed shut with a violent force and locked, trapping Steve in the bitter, sub-zero temperature, for which he was not properly dressed. Steve attempted to make several outgoing calls on his cellphone, but reception in the building has always been notoriously bad. After no luck of getting through to anyone, Steve, in a state of complete panic, began pounding incessantly on the closed door. "Help! Someone please help me! I'm stuck! Ed, are you there?! Please help me!" Just as Steve uttered his last word, a loud scratching sound filled the lobby. Frantically searching for where the sound was coming from, he noticed a column sliding down the adjacent wall. Suddenly, BAM! The rough end of the column directly struck Steve's shin, ripping the skin off his leg nearly to the bone. Steve dropped to his good knee in agony, shivering uncontrollably, as the frigid air ripped through his body. Ed finally heard Steve as he let out another desperate yell for help and came bursting through the door. Steve, feeling relieved that someone came to his aid, hobbled back to the office, where he warmed up and administered first aid to his leg. He decided to upload his cellphone photos to the computer, discovering a looming shadow person standing alongside the column that had crashed to the ground. "I honestly believe what lurks within this building is out to hurt and scare people."

Jim's son, Zac Terebus, was only twelve years old when Erebus opened to the public. Currently, he serves as the operations manager but was not a believer in the paranormal until he began working in the building. "Growing up in the haunt industry, we always made the ghosts, so I did not believe in them. I was pretty excited when we organized for a paranormal team to come in and investigate." On Saturday, October 23, 2011, the Lower Michigan Paranormal Society (LMPS) arrived for their investigation at five o'clock in the morning and began setting up their equipment. The staff were feeling completely drained, as they had already worked a full twelve-hour day on their busiest night of the year, which surprisingly fell on Sweetest Day. Zac, as bone-weary as he was, volunteered to stay and oversee the ghost hunt. Hours went by, and as far as Zac was concerned, nothing remarkable was happening. The members of the LMPS spent an extended period in the boiler room, trying to elicit a response from the deceased homeless man. Zac, who was growing extremely bored, sat in the back of the room hoping for any activity. In a state of utter exhaustion and vexation, he screamed, "Turn the light on!" Lo and behold, Zac's flashlight that was resting on the ground turned on at his command. Everyone in the room turned around to look at Zac, and absolutely shocked, he shouted, "No way, man!" Keith Hembree, the group's founder, requested Zac ask more questions. "He apparently listens to you! Ask him to turn it off." Sure enough, when Zac asked for the flashlight to be turned off, it did so immediately. For fifteen minutes, Zac played with the entity, getting him to turn the flashlight on and off repeatedly. "I knew that no one was messing with me because it was my flashlight that was responding to the requests. The only way to turn it on or off is to physically push the button in, and I kid you not, we could hear it clicking on and off each time. That was it for me. I am a believer now, and that is my ghost story."

Jason Osterman, Joe Stanson and Michele Casey, other seasoned employees with Erebus, have had their own eerie encounters in the building over the decades that they have worked there.

Jason, the former head of construction, often brought his son, Paul Michael, and daughter, Taylor, to work with him. One cloudy spring day, Taylor was assisting her father with finishing up a wall in the newly renovated lobby. Out of nowhere, a wispy gray mass came into Jason's peripheral vision. Being no stranger to the dust and debris that occurs during renovation, Jason ignored the anomaly and quickly went back to his work. Out of the blue, Taylor cried out, "Dad, look!" Jason quickly turned to face his daughter as she lifted her shirt to reveal three jagged claw marks etched into her stomach. With tears in her eyes, Taylor exclaimed, "It burns!" Like any concerned parent, Jason began asking questions to try to find answers.

"Did you feel anything?"

"No, I just felt burning pain as I was standing here with you." Jason and Taylor quickly exited the lobby in pursuit of medical attention. Is it possible that Taylor's scratches were caused by the same evil entity that injured Steve? Not long after Taylor's incident, Jason and Joe, who works at the attraction as a maintenance man and electrician, had a horrifying experience within the boiler room with the building's resident phantom.

After a day of heavy rainfall, the guys went downstairs to assess any damage done. The boiler room was extremely dark, so Jason and Joe proceeded to turn on their flashlights. In one of the corners of the room opposite the petrified items sits a standing pit of water, and the guys watched as water continually flowed into it from the outdoors. As Joe stood on the right, fixated on the amount of water flowing in, Jason shone his flashlight to the left toward a pillar that stood next to the abandoned belongings on the floor. As he scanned the fourteen-foot gap between the ground and ceiling with his eyes, he could see what appeared to be the silhouette of a human head emerging sideways from behind the pillar about eight feet into the air. It quickly disappeared behind the support beam just as fast as it appeared. Jason instantly took off running, with Joe trailing behind him shortly thereafter. "Jason, why are we running?" Joe asked, startled. In the distance Jason could be heard yelling, "Just run!" Joe did not see the shadow that evening but has seen the shadow figure almost daily since he began working for the Terebus brothers in May 2008. "I work out of a key room in the shop area of the basement. Originally, the room was used by management in the 1920s. Every time I work, I see a tall shadow figure emerge from a window on the wall." Even though the entity interacts with people, Joe also believes the entity has some residual qualities. "In spite of the area being very well lit, a six-to-seven-foot opaque humanoid shape just comes out of nowhere. Every time I have seen it, it always tends to move in the same direction, traveling northwest about ten feet until it just fades off. I see it all the time and always in the same manner." With many late nights spent at the haunt,

Joe has driven his Ford Explorer into the building to sleep instead of driving home to Brighton. On one occasion, he experienced something so profound that he still cannot identify what it was or what had caused it.

While in the shop, Joe lost track of time while removing and doing repair work on the transmission of his vehicle. When he glanced at the clock, he muttered some expletives to himself, realizing that he worked far too long into the wee hours of the morning and had to be back at work at 9:00 a.m. Far too tired to drive home, Joe locked the doors to his vehicle and proceeded to put the seats down in the back of his truck and lay out his sleeping bag. As he attempted to get comfortable, he lay in the eerie silence of the parking garage beneath the moonless sky. After finally succumbing to exhaustion, Joe passed out into a deep sleep, only to be woken up by a light at three o'clock in the morning.

This time was referred to in medieval times as the devil's hour based on religious scripture. The belief is that because Jesus was crucified at 3:00 p.m. and 3:00 a.m. is the opposite of that, this hour makes individuals more susceptible to experiencing demonic activity. The Catholic Church even prohibited any activities from taking place between 3:00 a.m. and 4:00 a.m. If a woman was caught engaging in any social activities from midnight to 4:00 a.m., she was shamed and labeled a witch—hence the phrase "witching hour." This phrase first appeared in literature in 1793. It is believed by many that spirits, especially inhuman ones, are at their strongest and the veil between the living and the dead is at its thinnest.

The entire inside of Joe's Explorer was glowing bright red, and while he found it odd, being skeptical, he began to mentally troubleshoot the electrical systems in the building, trying to come up with an explanation for the light. When he struggled to come up with an explanation regarding the electrical systems, he began thinking perhaps his brake lights were on but then questioned why his brake lights would be on in the first place. A shadow appeared to have been being cast from this light, but where the light source was coming from remained unknown. Lying on his right side, Joe decided to follow the light to the left. Through his back window, he could clearly see a fiery self-illuminating sphere the size of a softball slowly floating behind his vehicle. The orb was bright and emitted so much light that it had illuminated the entire area of the shop that surrounded it. Joe watched in a state of both amazement and terrorizing fear. "I was so afraid I could not move any part of my body. I have never seen anything like that before in my entire life. It was incredible." The crimson sphere floated around to Joe's left window. Hysterically, Joe exclaimed, "This is not happening!" He shut his eyes as tight as he could, wishing the ball of light would disappear. When he opened his eyes again, the shop lights were on and it was ten o'clock in the morning. Although it sounds as if Joe simply had a nightmare or was experiencing hallucinations, he stands behind his story. "I know it sounds absolutely crazy, but it happened. I would put my hand on a Bible over it. I remember so vividly how the experience made me feel—absolutely frozen in fear and totally shocked at what had just occurred."

Despite Erebus being such a spooky place to work, the turnover rate for year-round employees is shockingly low. However, there have been seasonal employees who have refused to ever come back after encountering the evil presence that resides within the building. There have been numerous claims by actors of being pushed, shoved and grabbed by unseen hands and coming face to face with the menacing shadow figure while they stood alone in their designated spots. One notable incident happened during a previous haunt season and occurred right before the doors opened to the public. Ed was doing a walkthrough of the structure, making sure the actors were in their places and all was ready to go. When passing by a section of the haunt with a dropping bridge, Ed noticed the actor assigned to that specific area was missing. Frustration and confusion consumed Ed's mind. "I just kept thinking to myself, *Where the hell is he?* He was absolutely nowhere to be found!" Just as Ed was about to turn and walk away to continue searching for the missing actor, he spotted a slight movement on the ground. Glancing down, he noticed the actor was laying flush against the floor on his back, taking slow and shallow breaths. "What the heck are you doing down there? You must stay in your spot. People will be entering the haunt at any minute now." The actor looked up timidly at Ed, as he anxiously replied, "I'm hiding, Ed. I'm hiding." His body was trembling uncontrollably. A black mass had appeared a few feet in front of the actor before taking on a large humanoid shape and storming toward him with an unrelenting anger. The actor's first instinct was to drop to the ground and try to blend in with the darkness. The idea of having to encounter the shadow figure again was so daunting to the actor that he ended up leaving his position at Erebus that very night.

In addition to reports of malevolent activity, sounds of whispers in both ears simultaneously and electrical appliances malfunctioning are just one more facet of the haunted happenings that plague Erebus. Many attribute the accumulated energy to the Clinton River, which runs beneath downtown Pontiac. If that's the case, it appears that no area of the haunt is safe from the ominous presence that prowls within.

Office administrator Michele Casey refuses to walk through the building, spending all her time in the office plastered with different covers of *Fear Finder* magazine and media articles featuring the haunt. It's the least daunting room in the facility. But even Michele has a story about something that has made her hair stand on end. Twice while sitting at her desk, which faces the hallway door, she observed two shadow anomalies passing by the door's vertical windowpane. Another time, she sat at her desk as a black shadow darted across the floor toward her. Almost sounding betrayed by the creepy encounters, she stated, "I felt like I would be protected in the office, but that was not the case."

Since the Erebus Haunted Attraction opened, it has captivated worldwide attention with its many accomplishments. In August 2005, the haunt was the first U.S. creation to make the *Guinness Book of World Records* for the world's longest walk-through haunted attraction. They maintained that title until September of 2009. In 2009, the Terebus brothers even had the opportunity to work on an American-style haunt, Shanghai Nightmare, in China for a season. In 2019, Erebus was ranked the no. 1 haunted attraction in the country by *USA Today* readers. The haunt has even been featured on various

The four-story haunt has been ranked as top in the nation. *Author photo.*

television shows. Every year, an impressive production is put on during the Halloween season, but nothing beats the amazing crew behind it all. The staff participates annually in a national anti-bullying campaign called "Don't Be a Monster," in which they travel to different schools promoting acceptance and unity among youth. It's a haunt that delivers year after year in more ways than one.

From the red-faced horned gargoyle that greets people into the haunt to the four floors of man-made chaos AND the unpredictable paranormal happenings, one thing is for sure—Erebus is a thrill seeker and paranormal enthusiast's perfect paradise. Steve Shipp agrees. "I do not scare easily, but every day when I get to work, I go straight into my office and pray out loud. This is the only place where I can look into the darkness and feel it looking back at me."

CONCLUSION

No matter what location you visit across the world, it seems that at least one person has a ghost story about that place. Fortunately for me, Detroit ghost stories and legends are plentiful. Obviously, with that being the case, finding content pertaining to Detroit being haunted was not the hard part. Selecting which local legends and places to feature in the book was. Many Detroiters already know the story of the Nain Rouge and have heard the story countless times. But what would a haunted Detroit book be without including the city's oldest legend? And while it may be that a great portion of Detroiters already know that story like the back of their hands, there are still those who have never heard it before. I wanted to include a mixture of stories that were widely known within the paranormal community and others that were not. Between Detroit and its many surrounding suburbs, certainly my work was cut out for me when I took on this project. Honestly, this book could have been never-ending based on the amount of content I obtained when doing my research.

The question I get asked the most whenever people discover that I am an author of paranormal regional history books is, "So you write fiction and just make up the ghost stories as you go?" To which I reply, "Absolutely not." With each chapter I have done extensive research on the history of every location and worked directly with at least one individual who is a staff member or volunteer from the haunted location. I also used my social media accounts to try to find individuals willing to share their paranormal experiences with me. Some people were more confident about sharing their stories, and others preferred to remain anonymous for fear of judgment. I am thankful to everyone who was courageous enough to share their story, whether they chose anonymity or not, because without them, this book simply would not exist.

Author Nicole Beauchamp standing in the parking lot of the Leland Hotel, with a view of Downtown Detroit in the background. *Courtesy of Jay Itchon (Misanthropia Narcissus).*

With this book, I wanted to not only relay some of the most amazing paranormal stories I had ever heard but also capture the essence of Detroit. Detroit is a grossly misunderstood city, but it really is beautifully diverse and incredibly eventful. Its many people are hardworking, creative and kind. It is also a city that exhibits remarkable resilience. Nothing holds this city back, and nothing ever will. Being born and raised in Bay City, Michigan, I feel absolutely honored to have had the support of so many Metro-Detroiters with this project. Hopefully I did those who entrusted me with their true paranormal accounts proud.

From the tragic tales within the text to the painful loss of a local Detroit hero, Ed Steele Jr., while writing the book, this project has taught us that life is far too short to take for granted. Love deeply, and be kind always. You just never know what someone else may be going through or how long they have left on this Earth. It is my goal that this book not only inspires others to visit Detroit and support the local businesses featured within but also gives people the hope and courage to chase their own dreams and seize every opportunity that comes their way, just like Ed did.

Even though 74.6 percent of Americans believe in something paranormal according to a 2017 Chapman University survey, there are still many people out there who are highly skeptical or undecided. Perhaps they have yet to have their own experience. While I am not out to convince anyone to believe in any certain way, I hope I can broaden your perspective. After all, you must admit it is a bit paranormal to think about how we are just chilling on a rotating planet that is floating in a huge galaxy within a massive universe. But here we are, killing it. Stay receptive to the mysteries of the world that you do not fully understand, and as Eminem said best in the letter he wrote to his beloved city, "Stay up, Detroit."

BIBLIOGRAPHY

Adkins, Jeff, and Todd Bonner. *America's Most Terrifying Places*. "Ghost Cops." Travel Channel. https://www.detroitparanormalexpeditions.com/tvshows.

American Hauntings. "Evangelista Occult Murders." Accessed June 4, 2021. https://www.americanhauntingsink.com/evangelista.

Ancarana, Angela. "HAUNTED HISTORY 3:00 a.m.—The Witching Hour." IHorror. February 10, 2021. Accessed September 10, 2021. https://www.ihorror.com/haunted-history-300-a-m-the-witching-hour/.

Austin, Dan. "Leland Hotel: Historic Detroit." Historic Detroit. Accessed April 15, 2021. https://historicdetroit.org/buildings/leland-hotel.

Ave-Lallemant, Dale. "The Red Devil of Detroit." Wyandotte, MI Patch. June 23, 2011. Accessed April 07, 2021. https://patch.com/michigan/wyandotte/bp--the-red-devil-of-detroit.

Bartkowiak, Dave, Jr., and Nick Monacelli. "Man Killed in Fire at the Leland Apartments in Downtown Detroit." WDIV. July 19, 2018. Accessed April 15, 2021. https://www.clickondetroit.com/news/2018/07/19/man-killed-in-fire-at-the-leland-apartments-in-downtown-detroit/.

Baulch, Vivian M. "Tales from the Crypts: Elmwood Cemetery Stories." *Detroit News*, June 21, 2013. https://www.loststory.net/history/tales-crypts-elmwood-cemetery-stories.

Bielski, Ursula. *Haunts of the White City: Ghost Stories from the World's Fair, the Great Fire and Victorian Chicago*. Charleston, SC: The History Press, 2019.

Blackmon, Caroline. "17 Facts You Might Not Know about Detroit." *Detroit Free Press*. July 20, 2018. Accessed April 4, 2021. https://www.freep.com/story/news/local/michigan/detroit/2018/07/20/facts-detroit-birthday/796115002/.

Bozick, John, Emily Fisher and Lucas Resetar. "Fort Wayne: Exploring History From Its Construction to the Modern Day." DetroitIsIt. March 10, 2021. Accessed August 03, 2021. https://detroitisit.com/fort-wayne-history-construction-modern-day/.

Brown, Jocelynn. "101 Years Ago: When the Spanish Flu Ravaged Detroit." *Detroit News*, April 5, 2020. Accessed August 19, 2021. https://www.detroitnews.com/story/news/local/detroit-city/2020/04/04/looking-back-on-spanish-flu-ravaged-detroit-coronavirus-pandemic/5087043002/?fbclid=IwAR3T3_bDG0sjgbco5hmzcyUZEvbSm9zTLqrjR6-T3usC3uWctgY56obDdFE.

Bulanda, George. "The Way It Was—The Leland Hotel, 1940." *Hour Detroit*, September 4, 2019. Accessed April 15, 2021. https://www.hourdetroit.com/the-way-it-was-articles/the-way-it-was-the-leland-hotel-1940/.

Burtka, Brian. "Montgomery C. Meigs and Fort Wayne." Military History of the Upper Great Lakes. October 22, 2017. Accessed August 03, 2021. https://ss.sites.mtu.edu/mhugl/2017/10/22/montgomery-c-meigs-fort-wayne/.

Camero, Gabriel. "I Ain't Afraid of No Ghosts." The South End. October 23, 2013. Accessed August 17, 2021. https://www.thesouthend.wayne.edu/features/article_fa2fb244-3cdb-11e3-9e02-001a4bcf6878.html?fbclid=IwAR2hEvaINEizklA_w5iyUDL8AAn7RNQtz9E9F9yS5KCC7KezFuE14ZRdT5k.

The Canadian Encyclopedia. "Antoine Laumet, Dit De Lamothe Cadillac." Accessed April 04, 2021. https://www.thecanadianencyclopedia.ca/en/article/antoine-laumet-cadillac?fbclid=IwAR3p0e2SeumveXjOt3HrTEIcrcZPtqRJ4Ck2eZNMjkYedTodU7hZRpSlLA8.

Canadian Museum of History. "The Explorers." Accessed April 4, 2021. https://www.historymuseum.ca/virtual-museum-of-new-france/the-explorers/antoine-laumet-dit-de-lamothe-cadillac-1694-1701/.

Centers for Disease Control and Prevention. "1918 Pandemic (H1N1 Virus)." March 20, 2019. Accessed August 21, 2021. https://www.cdc.gov/flu/pandemic-resources/1918-pandemic-h1n1.html.

City Club. "History." Accessed April 15, 2021. http://www.lelandcityclub.net/history.php.

Cold Cases Hard Copy. "Divine Profetil, Author and Private History Writer: The Life, Work and Murder of Benny Evangelist and His Family." Accessed June 4, 2021. http://coldcaseshardcopy.blogspot.com/2011/07/divine-profetil-author-and-private.html.

Connelly, Emily. "If Walls Could Talk." The South End. September 9, 2016. Accessed May 1, 2021. https://www.thesouthend.wayne.edu/features/article_bccc3c4e-6819-11e6-9f93-6b3ed6591e5d.html.

Detroit AllyCat. "Spooky Saturday Presents the Haunted Leland Hotel in Detroit, Michigan." Accessed April 18, 2021. https://www.youtube.com/watch?v=9yXd4x6xki0.

Detroit Book Fest. "Coolest Archives." Accessed August 20, 2021. https://detroitbookfest.com/tag/coolest/.

Detroit Free Press. "Grieving Father Leaps to Death." January 3, 1966.

———. "Hotel Death in City Stirs Police Probe." September 15, 1946.

———. "Hotel Death of Banker Called Suicide." July 30, 1949.

———. "Injured in Fall." August 14, 1938.

————. "Parents Leave Waifs to Starve on Streets." November 13, 1931.

————. "Police Look for Motive in Fatal Fall." July 29, 1949.

————. "Salesman Plunges 12 Floors to Death." September 26, 1942.

Detroit Historical Society. "Cadillac, Antoine de la Mothe." Encyclopedia of Detroit. Accessed April 06, 2021. https://detroithistorical.org/learn/encyclopedia-of-detroit/cadillac-antoine-de-la-mothe.

————. "Detroit's Brewing Heritage." Encyclopedia of Detroit. Accessed May 18, 2021. https://detroithistorical.org/detroit-historical-museum/exhibitions/special-exhibitions/detroit's-brewing-heritage.

————. "Fort Wayne." Encyclopedia of Detroit. Accessed July 22, 2021. https://detroithistorical.org/learn/encyclopedia-of-detroit/fort-wayne.

————. "Founding of Detroit." Encyclopedia of Detroit. Accessed April 4, 2021. https://detroithistorical.org/learn/encyclopedia-of-detroit/founding-detroit.

————. "Hull, William." Encyclopedia of Detroit. Accessed August 2, 2021. https://detroithistorical.org/learn/encyclopedia-of-detroit/hull-william?fbclid=IwAR2VNATJQnioOIITc85hd1Gr3h8yK6tUSl2boykLc6EbsEUwzVnDnhmTHTM.

————. "Uprising of 1967." Encyclopedia of Detroit. Accessed April 7, 2021. https://detroithistorical.org/learn/encyclopedia-of-detroit/uprising-1967.

————. "Whitney, Jr. David." Encyclopedia of Detroit. Accessed May 1, 2021. https://detroithistorical.org/learn/encyclopedia-of-detroit/whitney-jr-david.

Detroit News. "When the Flu Ravaged the World." *Michigan History*, June 21, 2013. Accessed August 19, 2021. http://blogs.detroitnews.com/history/1996/08/30/when-the-flu-ravaged-the-world/?fbclid=IwAR3taqHPspGUZZIR_yFKYIPM-vGI8Y2rItytzxirNsvnNH6rfdPsY3X3FaA.

Detroit Police Department. "New Sixth Precinct Station Dedicated." Police News, December 1930, 12.

Detroit Public Library. "About." Accessed June 1, 2021. https://detroitpubliclibrary.org/about.

Detroit Zoo. "Home." October 9, 2020. Accessed April 4, 2021. https://detroitzoo.org/.

DeVito, Lee. "Michigan's Creepy Eloise Asylum Is Now Open for Tours, Could Become a Paranormal-themed Hotel." *Detroit Metro Times*, May 10, 2021. Accessed May 11, 2021. https://www.metrotimes.com/the-scene/archives/2019/10/17/michigans-creepy-eloise-asylum-is-now-open-for-tours-could-become-a-paranormal-themed-hotel.

DPL News. "A Monument on Woodward for 100 Years." Accessed June 1, 2021. https://detroitpubliclibrary.org/news/a-monument-on-woodward-for-100-years.

DPX. "Detroit Paranormal Expeditions." Accessed April 14, 2021. https://www.detroitparanormalexpeditions.com/.

Eloise Haunted Tours. "History." October 17, 2019. Accessed May 15, 2021. https://www.eloiseasylum.com.

Encyclopedia Britannica. "Battle of Lake Erie." Accessed August 2, 2021. https://www.britannica.com/event/Battle-of-Lake-Erie.

————. "Detroit Riot of 1967." Accessed April 14, 2021. https://www.britannica.com/event/Detroit-Riot-of-1967.

————. "Insulin Shock Therapy." Accessed May 12, 2021. https://www.britannica.com/science/insulin-shock-therapy.

————. "Jimmy Hoffa." Accessed April 18, 2021. https://www.britannica.com/biography/Jimmy-Hoffa.

————. "Lobotomy." Accessed May 12, 2021. https://www.britannica.com/science/lobotomy.

————. "Shock Therapy." Accessed May 12, 2021. https://www.britannica.com/science/shock-therapy-psychiatry.

Encyclopedia.com. "Antoine de Lamothe Cadillac." Accessed April 6, 2021. https://www.encyclopedia.com/people/history/us-history-biographies/antoine-de-la-mothe-cadillac.

Erebus Haunted Attraction. "Erebus History—About Erebus Haunted Attraction in Pontiac." August 27, 2019. Accessed September 10, 2021. https://hauntedpontiac.com/history-of-erebus/.

Evangelist, Benjamin. *The Oldest History of the World: Discovered by Occult Science in Detroit, Mich.* Edited by Jarett Kobek. United States: Resurrectionary Press, 2001.

Farmer's History of Detroit. "The River, Islands, Wharves and Docks, Streams and Mills." Accessed April 6, 2021. https://www.maritimehistoryofthegreatlakes.ca//Documents/farmer/default.asp?ID=s004.

Final Report Proposed Detroit-Leland Hotel Historic District. PDF. City of Detroit. Accessed April 18, 2021. https://detroitmi.gov/sites/detroitmi.localhost/files/2018-08/Detroit-Leland%20Hotel%20HD%20Final%20Report.pdf.

Find a Grave. "Eliza Cameron Davenport Waterman (1827–1865)." Accessed May 23, 2021. https://www.findagrave.com/memorial/91653122/eliza-cameron-waterman.

————. "Elsie Wolwine." Accessed August 20, 2021. https://www.findagrave.com/memorial/11914396/elsie-wolwine.

Ford Corporate. "Henry Ford Biography." Accessed April 11, 2021. https://corporate.ford.com/articles/history/henry-ford-biography.html.

FOX 2 Detroit. "Nearly Three-Fourths of Americans Hold Paranormal Beliefs, Study Says." August 28, 2019. Accessed September 12, 2021. https://www.fox2detroit.com/news/nearly-three-fourths-of-americans-hold-paranormal-beliefs-study-says.

Frank, Annalise. "IT Entrepreneur, Owner of 'Haunted' Old Detroit Police Station Dies at 54." Crain's Detroit Business. August 27, 2021. Accessed September 1, 2021. https://www.crainsdetroit.com/obituaries/ed-steele-it-entrepreneur-owner-haunted-old-detroit-police-station-dies-54.

Gittleman, Stacy. "'Michigan Haunts' Details Eerie Spaces in Michigan—Detroit Jewish News." *Detroit Jewish News*, October 31, 2019. Accessed May 6, 2021. https://thejewishnews.com/2019/10/31/michigan-haunts-details-eerie-spaces-in-michigan/.

Haddad, Ken. "Michigan's Most Haunted: Eloise Psychiatric Hospital." WDIV. October 24, 2016. Accessed May 14, 2021. https://www.clickondetroit.com/features/2016/10/24/michigans-most-haunted-eloise-psychiatric-hospital/.

————. "St. Aubin Street Massacre: 1929 Detroit Family Murders Still Unsolved." WDIV. July 17, 2020. Accessed June 4, 2021. https://www.clickondetroit.com/features/2016/10/05/st-aubin-street-massacre-1929-detroit-family-murders-still-unsolved/.

Hamlin, Marie Caroline Watson. *Legends of Le Détroit*. Detroit, MI: T. Nourse, 1884.

Haunt Investigators of Michigan. *America's Most Terrifying Places*. "Restless Dead." Travel Channel. https://www.facebook.com/HauntInvestigatorsofMichigan.

Haymond, John A. "Laws of War." HistoryNet. February 12, 2019. Accessed August 15, 2021. https://www.historynet.com/laws-war-murky-line.htm?fbclid=IwAR1CCe4ru5hGZmjrizQXbsJm5oWeJQeG14-e6nP5GUxRTDI0yVNY9QffzO8.

Hembree, Keith. "About Paranormal Newz." Paranormal NewZ. Accessed September 8, 2021. https://paranormalnewz.weebly.com/about-paranormal-newz.html.

The Henry Ford. "Ford's Five-Dollar Day." *Past Forward*. January 3, 2014. Accessed April 11, 2021. https://www.thehenryford.org/explore/blog/fords-five-dollar-day/.

————. "Rosa Parks: What If I Don't Move to the Back of the Bus?" Accessed April 4, 2021. https://www.thehenryford.org/explore/stories-of-innovation/what-if/rosa-parks/.

Hester, Jessica Leigh. "The Spirited Afterlife of Detroit's Little Red Demon." Atlas Obscura. October 30, 2019. Accessed April 6, 2021. https://www.atlasobscura.com/articles/nain-rouge-detroit.

Historic Elmwood Cemetery & Foundation. "Where Detroit's History Endures." Accessed May 16, 2021. https://www.elmwoodhistoriccemetery.org/.

Historic Fort Wayne Coalition. "The Site's Significance to Native Americans." Accessed July 28, 2021. https://www.historicfortwaynecoalition.com/native_americans.html.

History.com. "Henry Ford." November 9, 2009. Accessed April 11, 2021. https://www.history.com/topics/inventions/henry-ford.

————. "Henry Ford Test-Drives His 'Quadricycle.'" November 13, 2009. Accessed April 4, 2021. https://www.history.com/this-day-in-history/henry-ford-test-drives-his-quadricycle.

————. "Tecumseh." November 9, 2009. Accessed August 2, 2021. https://www.history.com/topics/native-american-history/tecumseh?fbclid=IwAR1cEJfysh1w2chwYMY2lOCw5mGvwU6RHsQFzwNh6s5NpxluqMMIkwdDn8k.

————. "U.S. Surrenders Fort Detroit to the British." July 21, 2010. Accessed August 1, 2021. https://www.history.com/this-day-in-history/detroit-surrenders-without-a-fight.

The History of the Wayne County Poorhouse and Asylum - Eloise. Directed by Wayne Historical Society. Performed by Tyler Moll. YouTube. October 8, 2020. Accessed May 11, 2021. https://www.youtube.com/watch?v=OEucvjNT2sg&t=161s.

Ibbotson, Patricia. *Eloise: Poorhouse, Farm, Asylum, and Hospital (1839–1984).* Charleston, SC: Arcadia Publishing, 2002.

Jacobus, Donald Lines, and Edgar Francis Waterman. *The Waterman Family.* New Haven, CT: E.F. Waterman, 1939.

Johnson, Geoffrey. "The True Story of the Deadly Encounter at Fort Dearborn." *Chicago Magazine.* Accessed August 2, 2021. https://www.chicagomag.com/chicago-magazine/december-2009/the-true-story-of-the-deadly-encounter-at-fort-dearborn/?fbclid=IwAR2lWTd7OMtYIMo36rpLRGUQX1bOOE2hMx6xNCzIXwU0wvadgzZSJbMECyE.

Jones, Terry L. "Antoine De La Mothe, Sieur De Cadillac." *Country Roads*, March 26, 2018. Accessed April 4, 2021. https://countryroadsmagazine.com/art-and-culture/history/april-pastimes/.

Jorgenson, Dawn. "Elderly Man Injured When Nemo's Bar Bus Crashes in Downtown Detroit." WDIV. August 28, 2016. Accessed April 15, 2021. https://www.clickondetroit.com/news/2016/08/28/elderly-man-injured-when-nemos-bar-bus-crashes-in-downtown-detroit/.

Kelly, Kris. "The Spirits Are Haunting a Famous Detroit Landmark." CW50 Detroit. June 23, 2017. Accessed August 15, 2021. https://cwdetroit.cbslocal.com/2017/06/23/theyre-baa-aack-the-spirits-are-haunting-a-famous-detroit-landmark/.

Klein, Sarah. "Concierge Overkill." *Detroit Metro Times*, October 30, 2002. Accessed April 18, 2021. https://www.metrotimes.com/detroit/concierge-overkill/Content?oid=2174812.

Kuras, Amy. "7 Wonders of Detroit Public Library's Main Branch." Model D. Accessed June 1, 2021. https://www.modeldmedia.com/features/DPL-hidden-treasures-062315.aspx.

LaReau, Jamie L. "Mysterious Events, Bizarre Tales from Old Ford Plant Lead to Ghost Hunting Tours." *Detroit Free Press*, October 30, 2020. Accessed September 11, 2021. https://www.freep.com/story/news/local/michigan/detroit/2020/10/29/paranormal-ghosts-ford-piquette-plant/3749209001/.

The Making of the Modern U.S. "Ford's Impact." Accessed April 11, 2021. http://projects.leadr.msu.edu/makingmodernus/exhibits/show/henry-ford-assembly-line/impact-on-detroit#:~:text=This%20in%20turn%20created%20a,live%20in%20or%20around%20Detroit.&text=In%201930,%20at%20the%20building,57%%20over%20the%20decade3.

Marble, Jeremy. "A Video History of Detroit." Mlive. October 16, 2020. https://www.mlive.com/news/2020/10/a-video-history-of-detroits-nain-rouge.html.

Marklew, Tim. "A Brief History of the Leland Building." Culture Trip. March 12, 2018. Accessed April 18, 2021. https://theculturetrip.com/north-america/usa/michigan/articles/a-brief-history-of-the-leland-building/.

McFarlin, Jim. "Pontiac's Erebus the Setting for 'Ghost Stories' Saturday." *Detroit Metro Times*, September 8, 2021. Accessed September 11, 2021. https://www.metrotimes.com/table-and-bar/archives/2013/04/12/pontiacs-erebus-the-setting-for-ghost-stories-saturday.

McGraw, Bill. "Anti-Theft Door Trapped Young Brothers in Fire." *Detroit Free Press*, December 17, 1985.

Michael, Jason A. "Two Murders in Detroit." PrideSource. April 5, 2012. Accessed April 15, 2021. https://pridesource.com/article/two-murders-in-detroit-2/.

Michigan's Otherside. "The Red Dwarf of Detroit or the Nain Rouge." July 29, 2020. Accessed April 7, 2021. http://michigansotherside.com/the-red-dwarf-of-detroit-or-the-nain-rouge/.

Moye, David. "Want To See A Ghost? TV's 'Ghost Hunters' Reveal Top 3 Places to Look." *HuffPost*, December 28, 2011. Accessed August 5, 2021. https://www.huffpost.com/entry/ghost-hunters-water-limestone-railroad-tracks_n_1064457?fbclid=IwAR1aGOYbi88JbGafM47Rq7_q_2w_jMsPIX8cGHt_-3nNRUqLgBsfGsZryFw.

Nailhed. "Pleading the 6th." Accessed April 11, 2021. https://www.nailhed.com/2014/07/pleading-6th.html.

National Archives and Records Administration. "The Great Depression." Accessed April 12, 2021. https://hoover.archives.gov/exhibits/great-depression.

———. "Michigan SP Detroit—Leland Hotel." Accessed April 17, 2021. https://catalog.archives.gov/id/25341062.

National Parks Service. "Antoine De La Mothe Cadillac (U.S. National Park Service)." Accessed April 6, 2021. https://www.nps.gov/people/antoine-de-la-mothe-cadillac.htm.

———. "Fort Wayne: Detroit (U.S. National Park Service)." Accessed July 26, 2021. https://www.nps.gov/places/fort-wayne-detroit.htm.

Neavling, Steve. "Leland Hotel Fire Nearly Turned Catastrophic Because of Faulty Standpipes." *Motor City Muckraker*, December 10, 2014. Accessed April 18, 2021. http://motorcitymuckraker.com/2014/12/10/leland-hotel-fire-nearly-turned-catastrophic-because-of-faulty-standpipes/.

Oliver Hazard Perry Rhode Island. "Commodore Oliver Hazard Perry." February 12, 2020. Accessed August 2, 2021. https://www.ohpri.org/the-ship/commodore-perry/?fbclid=IwAR2HROQbPnFuB3hBmnKilNfUGWTX7gXGoRxgStzeN3l7o2PydcLWJEcsD0o.

PBS. "The Great Depression." Accessed April 11, 2021. https://www.pbs.org/wgbh/americanexperience/features/dustbowl-great-depression/.

Pedraja, Sierra. "Man Shot at Leland Hotel in Downtown Detroit after Argument." WDIV. February 18, 2017. Accessed April 20, 2021. https://www.clickondetroit.com/news/2017/02/18/man-shot-at-leland-hotel-in-downtown-detroit-after-argument/.

Pevos, Edward. "Michigan Haunted House, Ranked No. 1 in US, Opens This Week with COVID Changes." MLive. September 22, 2020. Accessed September 10, 2021. https://www.mlive.com/life/2020/09/michigan-haunted-house-ranked-no-1-in-us-opens-this-week-with-covid-changes.html.

Phantom for the First Course. Produced by Pilgrim Studios. Performed by The Atlantic Paranormal Society. Syfy, 2016. TV Show.

Psychiatry & Behavioral Health Learning Network. "Confronting Chaos." June 1, 2006. Accessed May 12, 2021. https://www.psychcongress.com/article/confronting-chaos.

Richardson, Gary. "Stock Market Crash of 1929." Federal Reserve History. Accessed April 12, 2021. https://www.federalreservehistory.org/essays/stock-market-crash-of-1929.

Rise Up Detroit. "The National Civil Rights Movement in Detroit—The North." February 20, 2019. Accessed April 4, 2021. https://riseupdetroit.org/chapters/chapter-3/part-1/the-national-civil-rights-movement-in-detroit/.

Risko, Karin, and Rodney L. Arroyo. *A History Lover's Guide to Detroit.* Charleston, SC: The History Press, 2018.

Robinson, John. "Michigan Legend: The Snake Goddess of Belle Isle." 99.1 WFMK. May 10, 2019. Accessed September 11, 2021. https://99wfmk.com/belle-isle-snake-goddess/.

Roney, Brendan. "The Battle of Bloody Run and Pontiac's Tree." Detroit Historical Society. July 31, 2015. Accessed May 18, 2021. https://detroithistorical.wordpress.com/2015/07/31/the-battle-of-bloody-run-and-pontiacs-tree/.

Saunders, Allison. "The Spirits of the Whitney's Ghost Bar." Opportunity Detroit. October 31, 2016. Accessed May 2, 2021. https://opportunitydetroit.com/blog/spirits-whitneys-ghost-bar/.

Solly, Meilan. "Rosa Parks' Detroit Home Is Now Up for Auction." Smithsonian. com. July 26, 2018. Accessed April 4, 2021. https://www.smithsonianmag.com/smart-news/rosa-parks-detroit-home-now-auction-180969763/.

Steele, Ed. Data Behind Bars. Accessed April 11, 2021. https://databehindbars.com/.

Tenney, John E.L. "St. Aubin's Street Massacre." St Aubins Street Massacre. January 13, 2016. Accessed June 5, 2021. http://benny.weirdlectures.com/2013/07/17/3587-st-aubin-avenue-then-and-now/.

Travel Through Time. "100 Years: Detroit and Prohibition." March 30, 2020. Accessed April 14, 2021. https://historynavigator.org/2020/03/18/100-years-detroit-and-prohibition/.

Turton, Jonathan. "We Went to 'America's Most Haunted Restaurant.'" Amuse. December 12, 2018. Accessed May 1, 2021. https://amuse.vice.com/en_us/article/qvqxgp/most-haunted-restaurant-america.

VR Preservation. "Burton Historical Collection." May 5, 2021. Accessed June 2, 2021. https://vrpreservation.org/burton-historical-collection/.

Walls, Dr. Bryan. "Freedom Marker: Integrity and Spirituality." PBS. Accessed April 4, 2021. https://www.pbs.org/black-culture/shows/list/underground-railroad/stories-freedom/abolition-slavery-canada/.

Wayne State University. "Rise Up Detroit Preserves the History of City's Civil Rights Movement." Today@Wayne. Accessed April 4, 2021. https://today.wayne.edu/news/2019/04/16/rise-up-detroit-preserves-the-history-of-citys-civil-rights-movement-31582.

Weird Detroit. "Ghost Story #5: Le Nain Rouge or a Mere Rogue Spirit?" Accessed April 6, 2021. http://weirddetroit.blogspot.com/2013/03/ghost-story-5-nain-rouge-or-mere-rogue.html.

"Westland, MI—Westland, Michigan Map & Directions." MapQuest. Accessed May 11, 2021. https://www.mapquest.com/us/michigan/westland-mi-282039251.

The Whitney Detroit. "About The Whitney." Accessed April 21, 2021. https://thewhitney.com/about.

"Who Killed the Evangelist Family?" Providentia. Accessed June 14, 2021. https://drvitelli.typepad.com/providentia/2018/11/the-evangelist-murders.html.

Wildt, Tanya. "Is Tommy's Detroit Bar & Grill Bar Haunted?" *Detroit Free Press,* October 30, 2014. Accessed September 11, 2021. https://www.freep.com/story/news/local/michigan/detroit/2014/10/30/tommys-detroit-bar-grill-haunted/18202035/.

Wisconsin Historical Society. "Iroquois Wars of the 17th Century." August 3, 2012. Accessed April 4, 2021. https://www.wisconsinhistory.org/Records/Article/CS385.

Zinn Education Project. "July 31, 1763: Chief Pontiac Wins Battle of Bloody Run at Fort Detroit." August 1, 2020. Accessed May 18, 2021. https://www.zinnedproject.org/news/tdih/battle-of-bloody-run/.

About the Author

Nicole Beauchamp is a native of Bay City, Michigan, and received her bachelor's degree in applied science from Siena Heights University in Adrian, Michigan. In addition to being an author, she also works as a Licensed Massage Therapist. With a lifelong passion for the paranormal and history, Nicole founded the Tri-City Ghost Hunters Society in 2009. Since forming the group, she has investigated all over the world. Over the years, she has presented at various libraries and universities within the state of Michigan with the goal of educating individuals on the paranormal and expressing the importance of preserving history through investigation. She has had the honor of co-lecturing with renowned paranormal researcher John E.L. Tenney, and her work has been featured in dozens of national and international publications. In 2015, she wrote a guest editorial for *TAPS ParaMagazine* and was featured on Beyond Reality Radio, where she was recognized for her hard work and dedication to the paranormal by Jason Hawes, the star of the popular television shows *Ghost Nation* and *Ghost Hunters*. In February 2019, she was featured on the cover of *Paranormal Underground* magazine. She received a tribute from the State of Michigan for her first book, *Haunted Bay City Michigan*, which was released in September 2020, and now offers paranormal tours of her hometown. Along with the paranormal, she loves traveling and animals. She hopes to continue to tour Michigan in order to enlighten individuals on the spirit realm.

Author photo copyright of Jay Itchon (Misanthropia Narcissus).